Oh, the doors you will open!

HARCOURT SCHOOL PUBLISHERS

STORYtown

Watch This!

Senior Authors
Isabel L. Beck • Roger C. Farr • Dorothy S. Strickland

Authors
Alma Flor Ada • Roxanne F. Hudson • Margaret G. McKeown
Robin C. Scarcella • Julie A. Washington

Consultants
F. Isabel Campoy • Tyrone C. Howard • David A. Monti

Harcourt
SCHOOL PUBLISHERS

www.harcourtschool.com

ISBN 10 0-15-343172-5
ISBN 13 978-0-15-343172-2

4 5 6 7 8 9 10 048 16 15 14 13 12 11 10 09 08

Watch This!

Harcourt
SCHOOL PUBLISHERS

www.harcourtschool.com

Theme 6
New Faces
New Places

Contents

Lesson 25

Get Started Story

Paired Selections

Student Writing Model: Personal Narrative

Science

4

BURTON'S FLYING CIRCUS

Science

Social Studies

Science

Science

Social Studies

Social Studies

Social Studies

Social Studies

Social Studies

Social Studies

Lesson 30

Theme Big Books

It Is the Wind
by Ronda Wolff
illustrated by
James Ransome

Here in Space

Written and illustrated by David Milgrim

READERS' THEATER
Harcourt School Publishers
Practice Book
Grade 1

The Thing Under the Bridge

Decodable Books 25–30

Comprehension Strategies

Before You Read

Look at the pictures.
Think about what
you already know.

9

While You Read

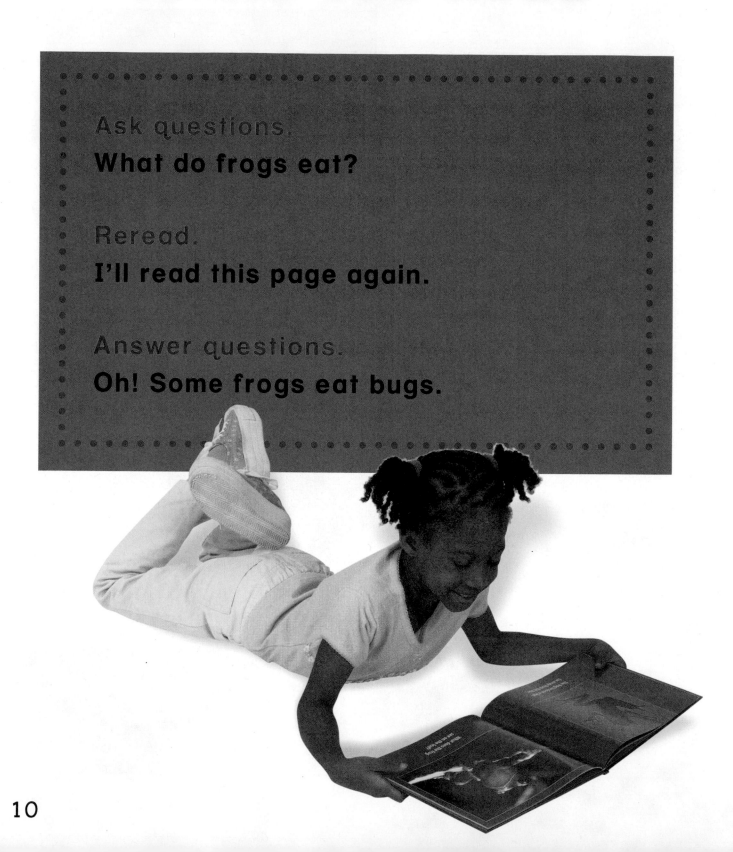

Ask questions.
What do frogs eat?

Reread.
I'll read this page again.

Answer questions.
Oh! Some frogs eat bugs.

After You Read

Retell.

First, tadpoles hatch from eggs.
Then, they begin changing into frogs.
Last, they are full-grown frogs.

Make connections.

This is like another book I read.
I learned how butterflies change.

Burton's Barnstormers,
Jane Wooster Scott

Contents

Lesson 25

1 Get Started **Story**

Duke's Work

by Sandra Widener
photographs by Eric Camden

2 Genre: Nonfiction

Amazing Animals

by
Gwendolyn Hooks

The Little Turtle

By Vachel Lindsay
Illustrated by Betsey Snyder

3 Genre: Poetry

15

Phonics

Words with <u>u-e</u>

Words to Know

Review

love

listen

because

visitor

Duke's Work

by Sandra Widener

photographs by Eric Camden

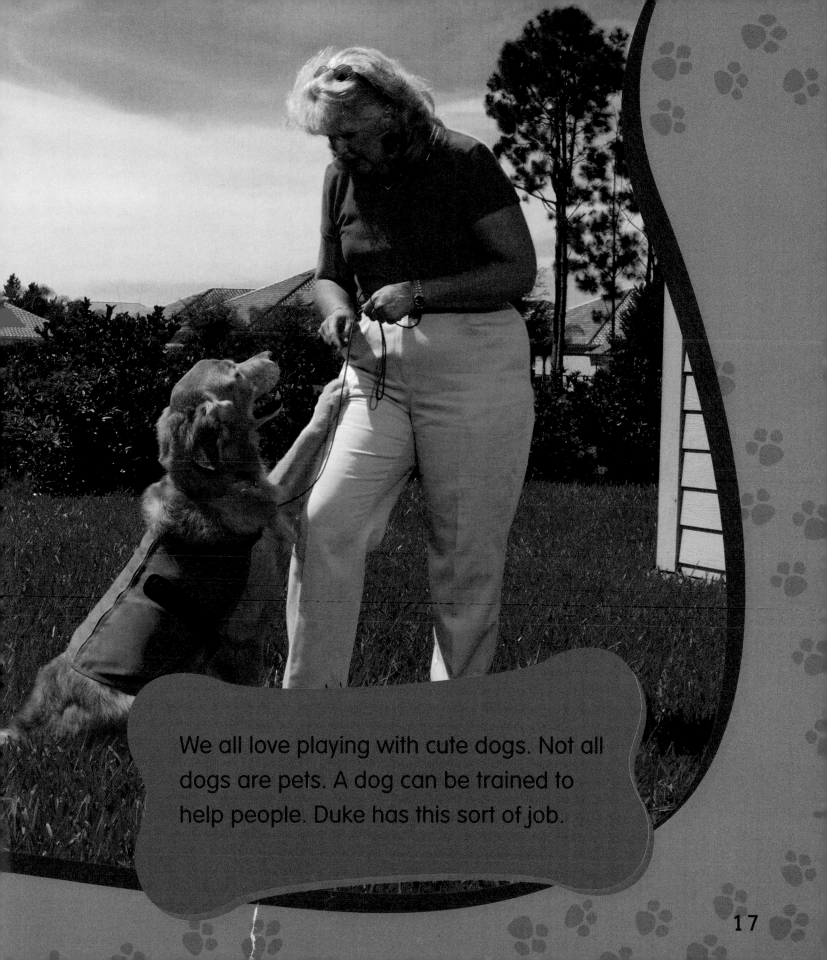

We all love playing with cute dogs. Not all dogs are pets. A dog can be trained to help people. Duke has this sort of job.

Duke is trained to listen because Mike cannot hear. Duke hears a visitor at the door. He tugs on Mike's hand. He has just told him he has a visitor.

Some dogs are trained and used as sled dogs. Sled dogs must be big and strong. They need thick fur to keep warm.

19

In cold places, roads may be lost under huge piles of snow. People use their sled dogs and sleds when they cannot use cars.

Other dogs are used for herding sheep.
The herd dogs keep the sheep safe. They
bark at the sheep to keep them close.

Those herd dogs make the sheep follow the rules. Herd dogs and other working dogs are used as partners and pets!

Dogs are fun, and dogs are good pets.
Dogs like Duke have jobs, but all dogs
like a big hug and lots of love, too!

23

Phonics Skill

Words with <u>u-e</u>

The letter **u**, followed by a consonant and **e**, can stand for the long <u>u</u> sound as in the words **mule**, **cute**, and **flute**.

mule

cute

flute

24

Look at each picture. Read the words.
Tell which word names the picture.

tube

tub

tribe

cope

cube

cub

GO online www.harcourtschool.com/storytown

Try This!

Read the sentences.

Bruce and June can play the flute. They know lots of good tunes. Bruce has a cute dog named Duke.

Words to Know

High-Frequency Words

- color
- hair
- clear
- toes
- kinds
- only
- good-bye

Hello! I am a polar bear. Look at the **color** of my **hair**. It looks white, but it is **clear**. I walk in the snow a lot. My **toes** are cold! I eat all **kinds** of fish. I have **only** one best friend. His name is Ice Bear. Well, it's time for me to go. **Good-bye**!

27

Amazing Animals
by
Gwendolyn Hooks

Nonfiction

Genre Study

In **nonfiction** the pictures and words work together to give information.

Animal	Special Feature	How it Helps

Comprehension Strategy

Use Graphic Organizers

Writing information on a graphic organizer will help you keep track of what you read.

Amazing Animals

by
Gwendolyn Hooks

Big eyes,
long beak,
thick fur,
big squeak!

Animals have many things
that help them live.

Polar Bear

A polar bear has thick fur. Each hair
is shaped like a tube. The hair is clear,
like glass. The sun makes it look white.

How does thick, white fur help?

Thick fur helps polar bears stay warm.
The color of their fur looks the same color
as snow. This helps them hide.

Where is this cute little polar bear hiding?

Elephant

An elephant has two long teeth and a long nose. The teeth are called tusks. The nose is called a trunk.

How do tusks and a trunk help?

33

Elephants use their tusks to scrape bark off trees. Then they eat the bark. Elephants use their trunk to get water.

Sometimes they spray water at each other!

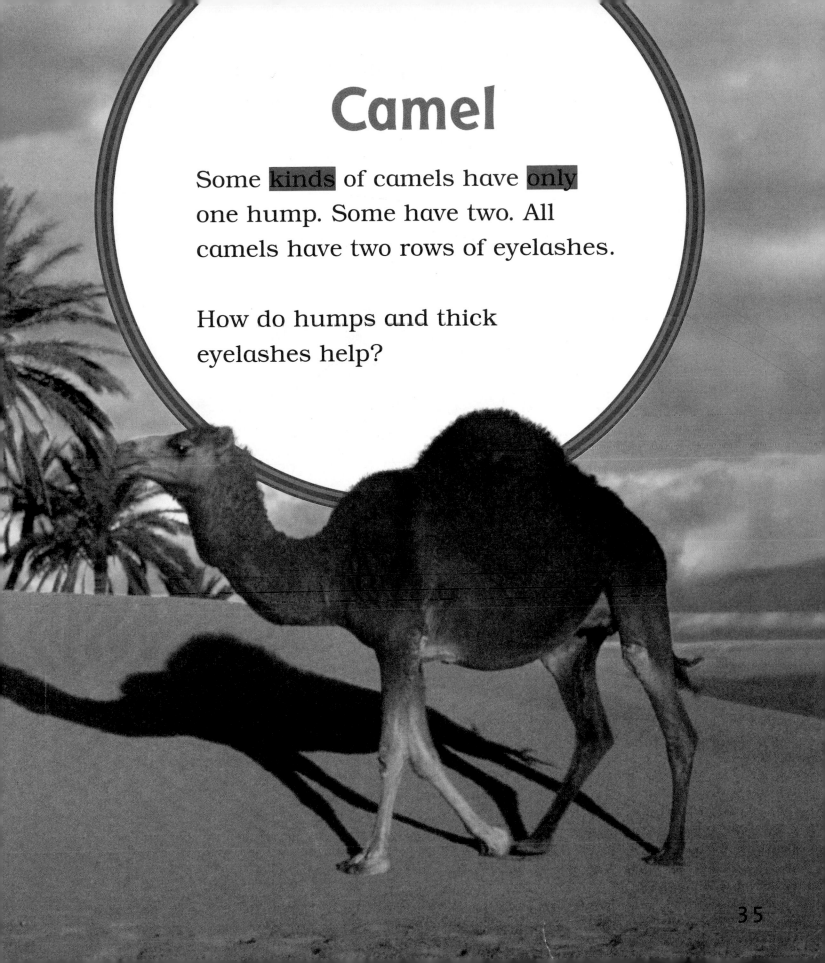

Camel

Some **kinds** of camels have **only** one hump. Some have two. All camels have two rows of eyelashes.

How do humps and thick eyelashes help?

A camel's hump has fat inside. On long trips, a camel's body uses the fat for food. A camel's eyelashes keep out the desert sand.

Look at these long eyelashes!

Duck

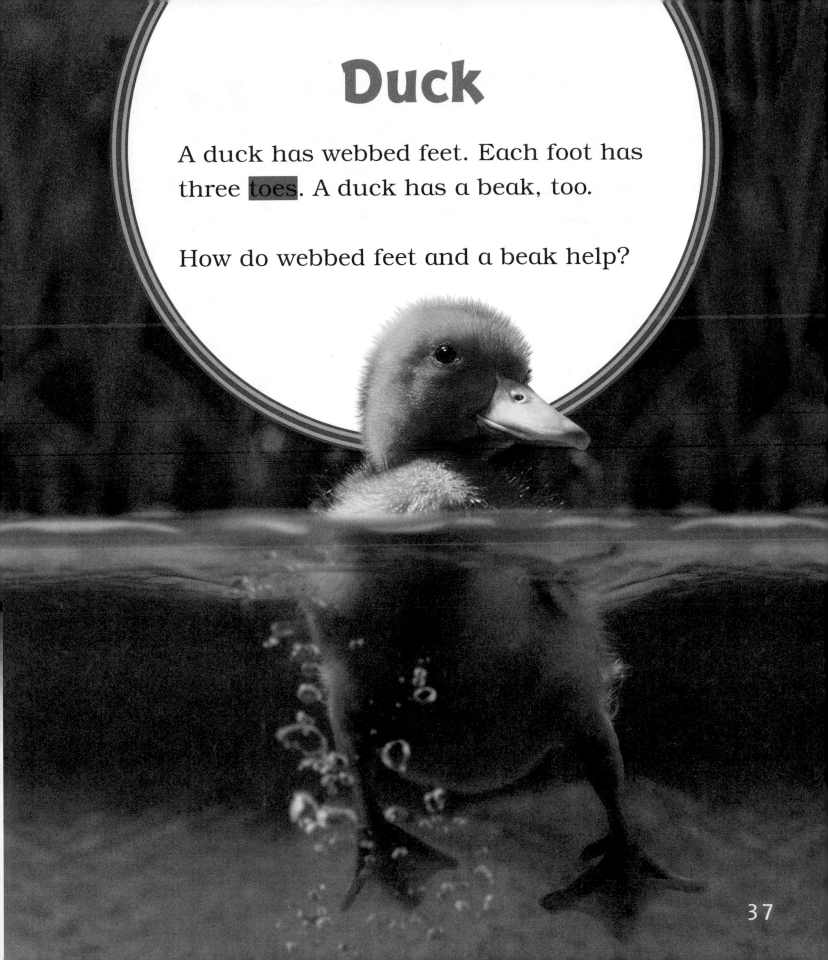

A duck has webbed feet. Each foot has three toes. A duck has a beak, too.

How do webbed feet and a beak help?

Ducks use their webbed feet as paddles.
Webbed feet help ducks swim fast.
Ducks use their beaks to eat plants.

This duck uses its beak to clean its
friend.

Giraffe

A giraffe has spots. A giraffe has a long neck.

How do spots and a long neck help?

A giraffe's spots help it hide. The giraffe's long neck helps it reach the leaves of trees.

This giraffe is bending her long neck down to kiss her little giraffe!

Porcupine

A porcupine has quills that are long and sharp.

How do quills help?

Quills help keep a porcupine safe. If an animal comes too close, the porcupine backs into it. The sharp quills hurt!

What might happen to this animal?

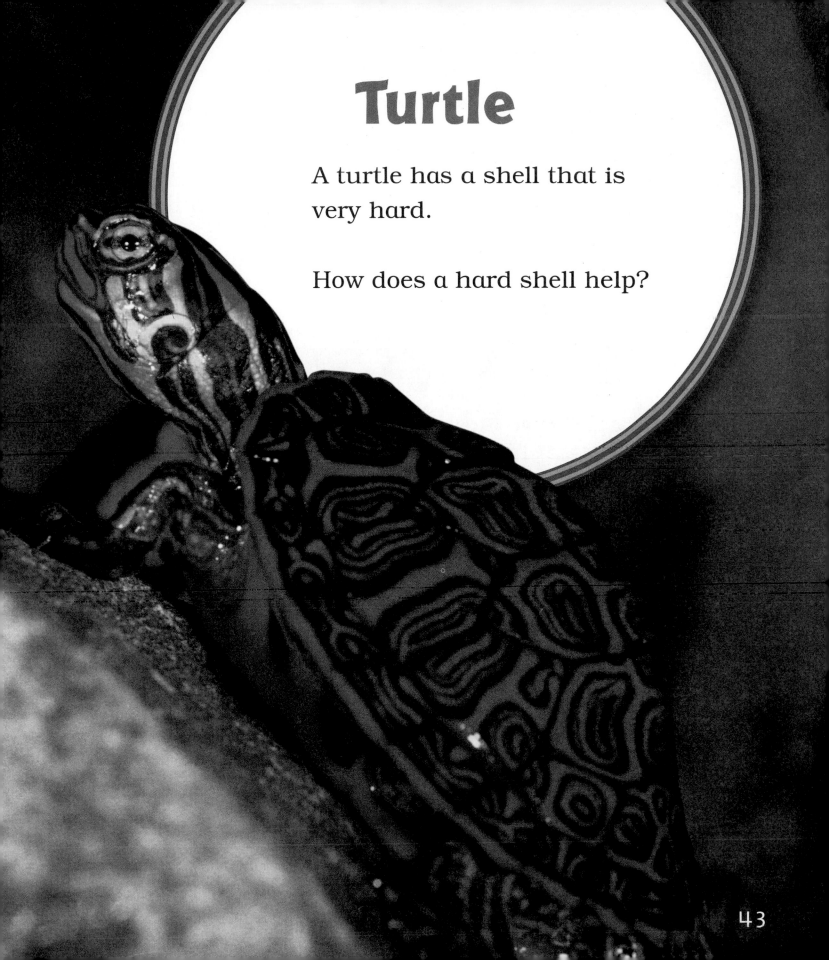

Turtle

A turtle has a shell that is very hard.

How does a hard shell help?

43

If an animal bothers a turtle, the turtle can go into its shell. When the animal goes away, the turtle comes back out.

Hello, turtle!

Dolphin

A dolphin's tail has two parts called flukes. A dolphin has two flippers.

How do tail flukes and flippers help?

A dolphin flips its tail flukes up and down to swim fast. It uses its flippers to turn to the left or right.

These two dolphins are swimming away.

Good-bye, dolphins!

Think Critically

1 Which animals have special things that help them to hide? 🐾 NOTE DETAILS

2 Which animals have special things that help them to eat? 🐾 NOTE DETAILS

3 What other things can elephants do with their trunks? DRAW CONCLUSIONS

4 Why do you think the title of the story is "Amazing Animals?"

MAKE INFERENCES

5 **WRITE** Which animal do you think is the most amazing? Write about it.

Meet the Author
Gwendolyn Hooks

Gwendolyn Hooks wrote this story because she loves animals. "This story is about wild animals," she explains. "I don't own any wild animals, but I do have a pet cat."

"I like writing nonfiction for children because real life is full of interesting facts.

If you want to be a writer, you should read every day. You can start your day by reading a cereal box!"

www.harcourtschool.com/storytown

The Little Turtle
By Vachel Lindsay
Illustrated by Betsey Snyder

Teacher Read-Aloud

Poetry

50

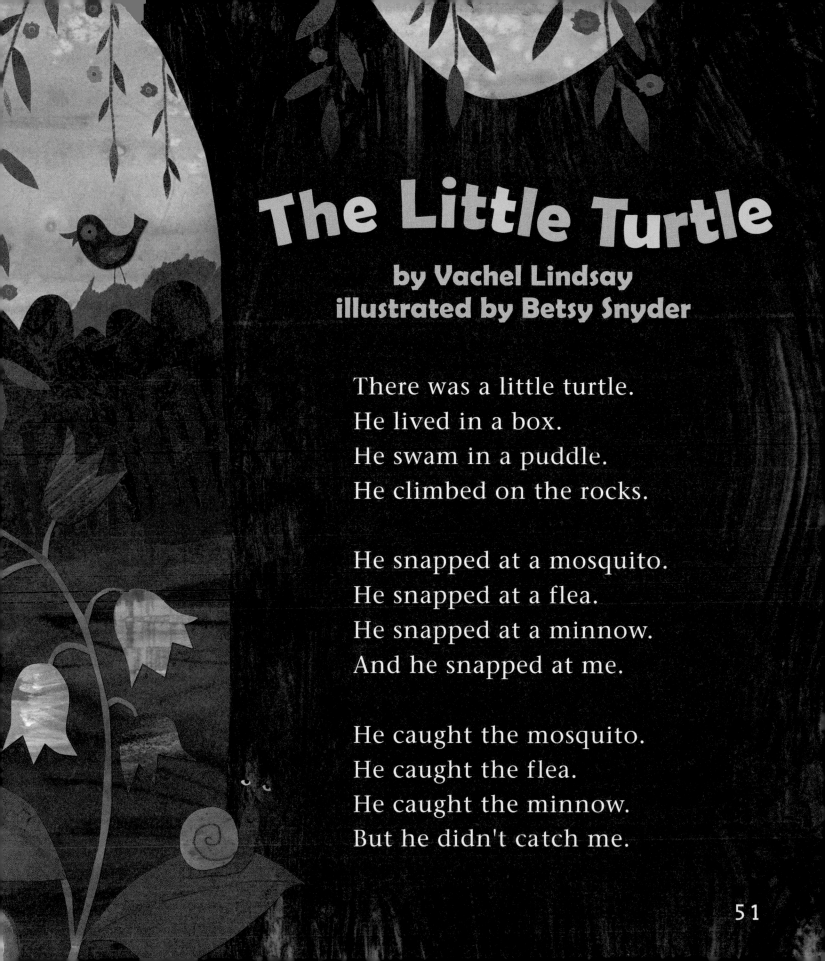

The Little Turtle

by Vachel Lindsay
illustrated by Betsy Snyder

There was a little turtle.
He lived in a box.
He swam in a puddle.
He climbed on the rocks.

He snapped at a mosquito.
He snapped at a flea.
He snapped at a minnow.
And he snapped at me.

He caught the mosquito.
He caught the flea.
He caught the minnow.
But he didn't catch me.

Connections

Comparing Texts

1 How are the selection and the poem the same? How are they different?

2 Tell about an amazing animal you have seen.

3 What is your favorite animal? Tell why.

Writing

Think of an animal you like. Look in a book for information about your animal. Write three facts about it.

A zebra is a mammal. It has black and white stripes. Zebras can run very fast.

Phonics

Make and read new words.

Start with <u>June</u>.

Change **J** to **t** .

Change **n** to **b** .

Change **t** to **c** .

Change **b** to **t** .

Fluency Practice

Read the story with a partner. Take turns reading each page. Read some pages as if you are reading to a baby. Read some as if you are reading to your teacher. Listen to how your voice changes!

Reading-Writing Connection

Personal Narrative

We have read many stories this year. "Mystery of the Night Song" is one of my favorites. Here is a story I wrote about me.

My story is called "The Painting Contest." I wrote a draft first. Then I made some changes.

Student Writing Model

The Painting Contest
by Abby

I love to paint! My dad knows this, so he got me a paint set. I painted a picture of my dog. Then I sent my picture to an art contest. I won! I was so happy.

Writing Trait

VOICE I begin by writing something that will make people want to read more.

Writing Trait

ORGANIZATION I write what happened in the beginning, in the middle, and at the end.

This is what I do when I write.

▶ **I write my ideas.**

camping trip

painting

visiting my
cousins

baking cookies

▶ **I choose the idea that I like best.**

▶ **I plan my story.**

> ## Beginning
> Dad gave me a paint set.
>
> ↓
>
> ## Middle
> I painted a picture for an art contest.
>
> ↓
>
> ## Ending
> I won the contest.

▶ **I write my ideas.**

▶ **I read my writing and make changes.**

▶ **I type my story on a computer.**

Here are some things to remember when you write a story about yourself.

Checklist for a Personal Narrative

☐ My story is about me.

☐ My story tells who, what, and when.

☐ My story has a beginning, a middle, and an ending.

☐ My sentences begin with capital letters.

☐ My sentences end with the right end marks.

☐ I use complete sentences.

Contents

Lesson 26

1 Get Started Story

Night Flight

by Emily Hutchinson
illustrations by Allison Jay

2 Genre: Fantasy

Blast Off!

Rozanne Lanczak Williams

Illustrated by
Pete Whitehead

3 Genre: Nonfiction Article

Traveling Through Time

Phonics

Words with y
and <u>igh</u>

Words to Know

Review

loudly

only

listen

clear

Night Flight

by Emily Hutchinson

illustrated by Allison Jay

"Fly away with me!" calls Dwight. "Let's leave this patch. You and I will fly like a butterfly!"

"Are you nuts?" Tyrone says loudly. "We can't
fly! We only have fur. We don't have wings! We
can't fly like a butterfly!"

62

"Listen, Tyrone," says Dwight. "You think we can't fly, but I have a surprise for you."

"What might that be?" asks Tyrone.

"Come with me," says Dwight. "I'll show you."

Dwight shows Tyrone what he has made.
The wings are made of bright nylon. The
frames are clear and light.

"We'll take our first flight at night," says Dwight.

"What a delight!" adds Tyrone. "It will be fun.
You and I will fly like a butterfly!"

That night, Tyrone and Dwight put the wings on tight. They leap off a high hill. It is a sight to see fur in flight!

66

"Oh, my! This is not right!" says Tyrone.
"I am not a butterfly!"

"No!" sighs Dwight. "We have fur, not
wings. Oh Well! We did try!"

Focus Skill

Plot, Setting, and Characters

The **plot** is what happens in a story. The **setting** tells where and when a story takes place. The **characters** are the people and animals in a story.

In the picture, the **plot** is about trying to go to the rainbow. The **setting** is over a forest in the daytime. The **characters** are a cat, a duck, and a bear.

Look at the picture. What is the plot? What is the setting? Who are the characters?

Try This!

Look at the picture. What is the plot? What is the setting? Who are the characters?

climbed

thought

Earth

fooling

table

Kim and Tyler loved to play in the park. They **climbed** to the top of a rocket.

"I am flying to the stars!" said Kim. "Now I am flying back to **Earth**."

"I **thought** this is just a pretend rocket," said Tyler.

"I'm just **fooling** around!" said Kim. "Let's fly to that **table** over there."

"Yes," said Tyler. "Let's go!"

 www.harcourtschool.com/storytown

Fantasy

Rozanne Lanczak
Williams

Pete Whitehead

Genre Study

A **fantasy** is a make-believe story. Fantasies often have animals that act like people.

Characters	Setting

Beginning

Middle

Ending

Comprehension Strategy

Monitor Comprehension: Adjust Reading Rate
If you don't understand what you are reading, you should slow down.

Blast Off!

by
Rozanne Lanczak Williams

illustrated by
Pete Whitehead

Kim and Tyler are good friends.

Their mothers are good friends, too.

One day, they all went to the park.

"I'll race you to the rocket ship!" cried Kim.

"On your mark, get set, go!"

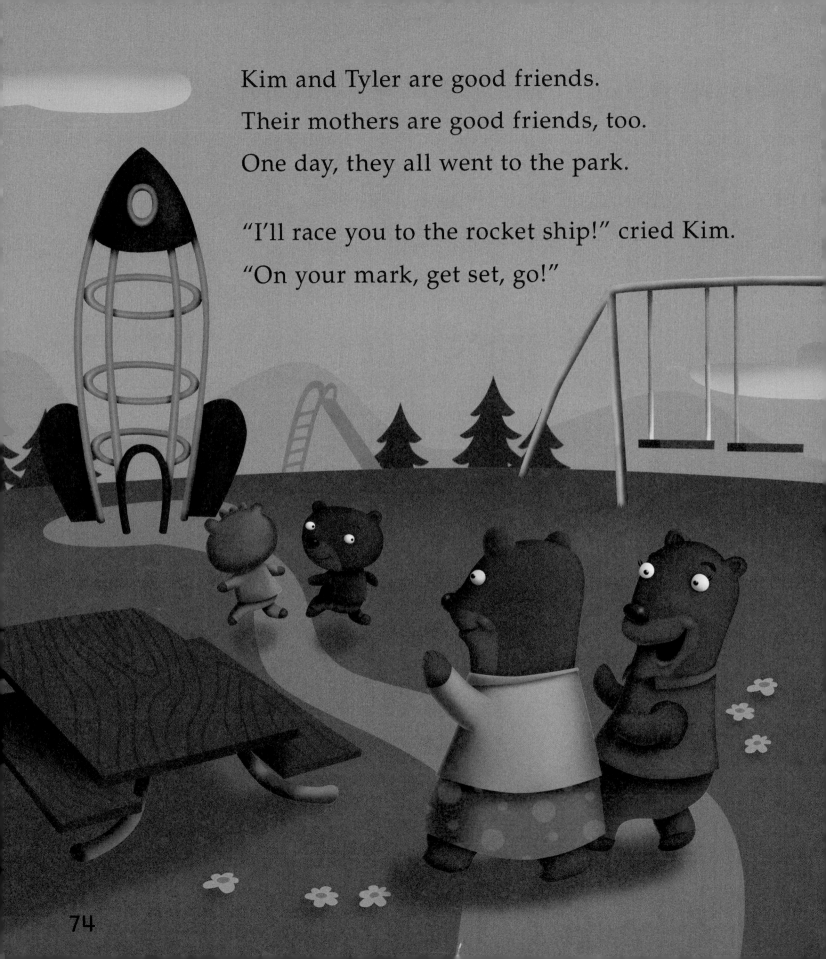

Kim and Tyler ran. They climbed to the top.
Their mothers sat at a picnic table.

"How fast do you think this thing can go?"
asked Kim.
"How far do you think it can go?"
asked Tyler.
"Let's try to turn it on!"
said Kim.

Tyler and Kim pushed every button. They flipped every switch. They turned every wheel.

"Let's go!" yelled Kim.

"10 - 9 - 8 - 7 - 6 - 5 - 4 - 3 - 2 - 1 . . . BLAST OFF!" they yelled.

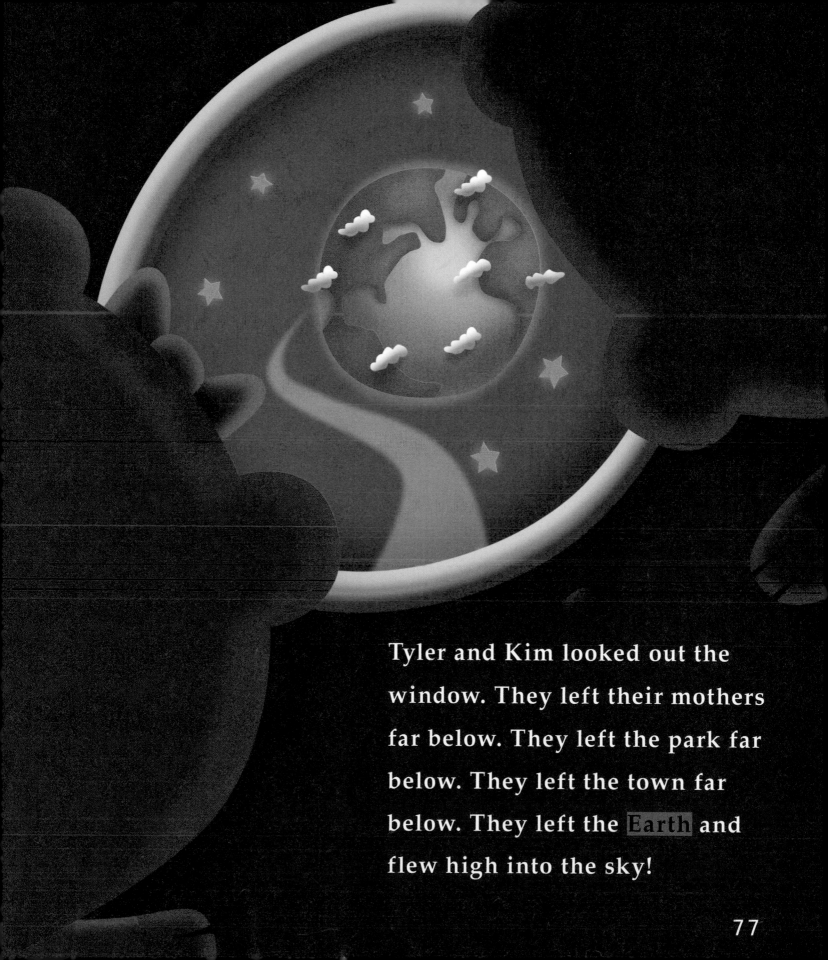

Tyler and Kim looked out the window. They left their mothers far below. They left the park far below. They left the town far below. They left the Earth and flew high into the sky!

They raced past the moon. They raced
past a comet. They raced past a star.
They raced to a bright
green planet.

"This is cool!" said Kim.

"What a sight!" said Tyler.

"Bleeble!" said a little green creature.

79

"I think Bleeble means hello," said Kim.

"I think you're right," said Tyler.

"Bleeble!" said Kim and Tyler.

The two friends played with the little green
creature. They swung on the swings. They
jumped, skipped, and climbed.

At last, Kim said, "Oh, no!
It's getting late. I think we
had better get back!"

"Zight zop!" said the little green creature.

"I think that means good-bye," said Tyler.

"I think you are right," said Kim.

"Zight zop!" said Kim and Tyler.

82

When Kim and Tyler got back, their mothers were still sitting there.

"Oh my, look at the time," said Kim's mother. "It's time for lunch!"

"We just flew to a bright green planet!" said Kim.

"Yes, and we met a new friend there!" said Tyler. "Didn't you hear our rocket blast off?"

"Well, yes. I thought I heard something," Kim's mother said with a wink.

"Are you two just fooling around?" asked Tyler's mother.

"Bleeble!" said Kim and Tyler.

"We have a surprise for you," said Tyler and Kim.

"Where did you get these?" asked Tyler's mother.

"Look at the green feathers!" said Kim's mother.

"Zight zop!" said Kim and Tyler.
They giggled and ran off to their rocket.

Think Critically

1 How would you describe Kim and Tyler? CHARACTERS

2 What are the two settings in the story? SETTING

3 What is the most important thing that happened? PLOT

4 Do you think that Kim and Tyler really visited another planet? MAKE INFERENCES

5 **WRITE** Write a new ending for "Blast Off!"

Meet the Author
Rozanne Lanczak Williams

Rozanne Lanczak Williams began writing stories when she was 8 years old. She says, "If you would like to be a writer, look around you and notice things. No one sees things just the way you do. Read lots of books! That's what inspires me."

Meet the Illustrator
Pete Whitehead

Pete Whitehead says that the best part about being an artist is drawing funny-looking characters. "For me, drawing animals is more fun than drawing people," he says.

 www.harcourtschool.com/storytown

89

Traveling
Through Time

Nonfiction Article

Traveling Through Time

Long ago, people had only their feet to carry them from place to place. Now, people ride in cars, trains, boats, and airplanes.

People have invented machines that can travel on land, in the water, and through the sky. People have even traveled all the way to the moon!

Buzz Aldrin on the ▶
Moon

**Look at some ways people in the past traveled.
Then, look at ways people travel in the present.**

**How do you think people will
travel in the future?**

Connections

Comparing Texts

1 How are the story and the article the same? How are they different?

2 Tell what you know about outer space.

3 Tell about an adventure you had.

Writing

Think about the story and the article. Look in a book for more information about outer space. Write three facts about it.

The Moon
Sometimes the moon looks round.

Phonics

Make and read new words.

Start with **tie**.

Change **i** **e** to **r** **y**.

Change **r** **y** to **i** **g** **h**.
Add **t** to the end.

Change the first **t** to **r**.

Fluency Practice

Some sentences need to be read loudly. Kim would say loudly, "I'll race you to the rocket ship!"

Look for sentences that should be read loudly. Look for some that should be read softly. Read them that way.

Contents

Lesson 27

Phonics

Words with <u>ou</u> and <u>ow</u>

Words to Know

Review

hear

kinds

remembered

clear

eyes

fooling

What Brad Found

by Linda Barr

illustrated by
Pablo Bernasconi

Brad sat on the couch reading.
He set his book down.

"What is that I hear outside?" he
asked. "It sounds like crying!"

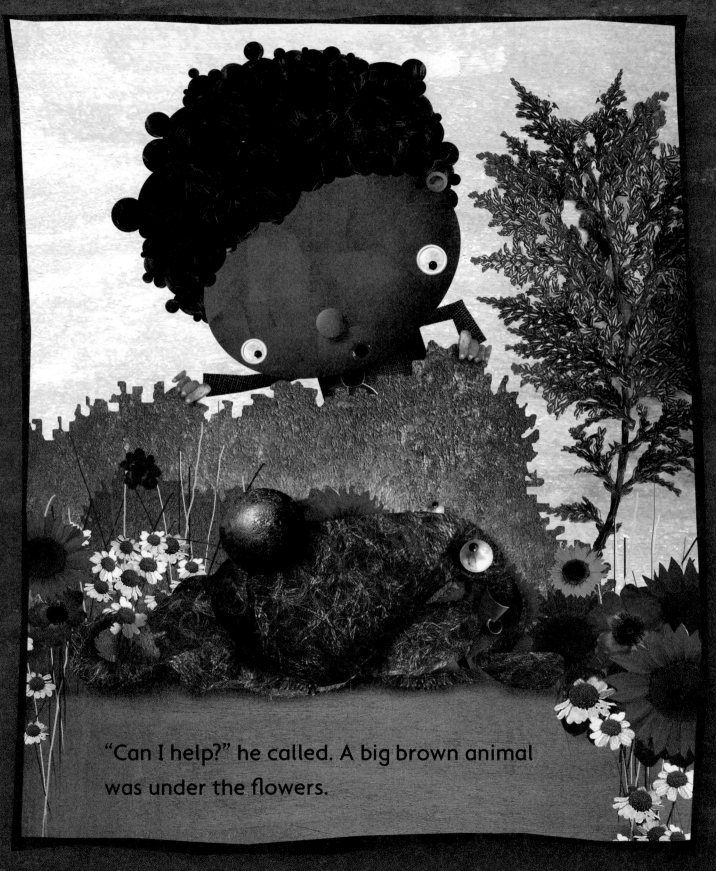

"Can I help?" he called. A big brown animal was under the flowers.

It was a dog!

"Are you lost?" Brad asked. The dog wagged its tail a thousand times.

Brad smiled. "You surprised me!"

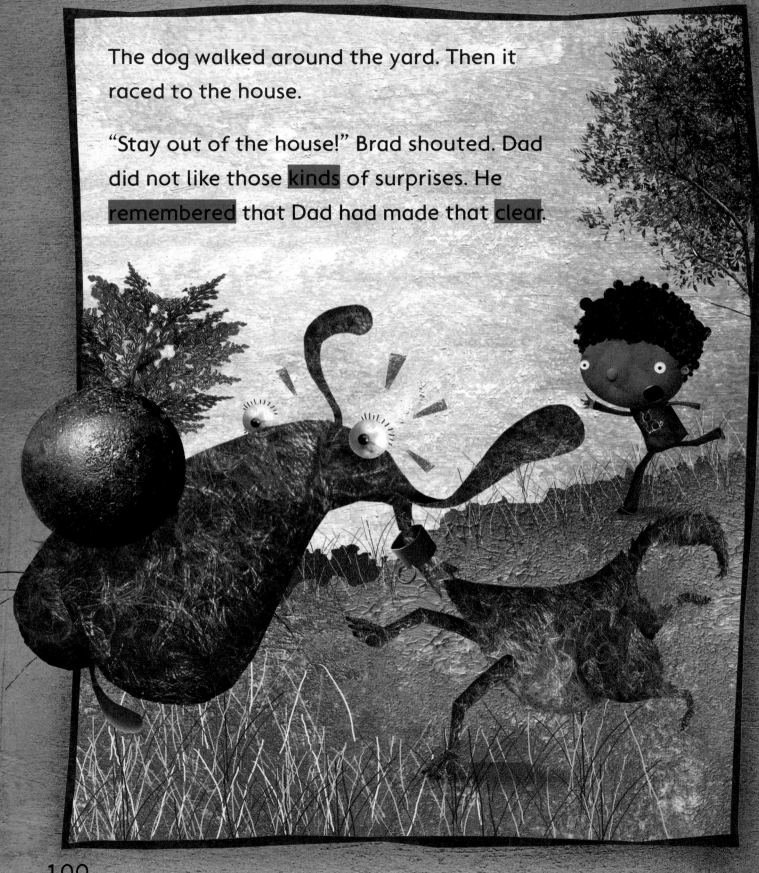

The dog walked around the yard. Then it raced to the house.

"Stay out of the house!" Brad shouted. Dad did not like those kinds of surprises. He remembered that Dad had made that clear.

Brad wanted to help the dog.
Maybe it didn't have a house.

Brad hoped Dad would let him
keep this dog.

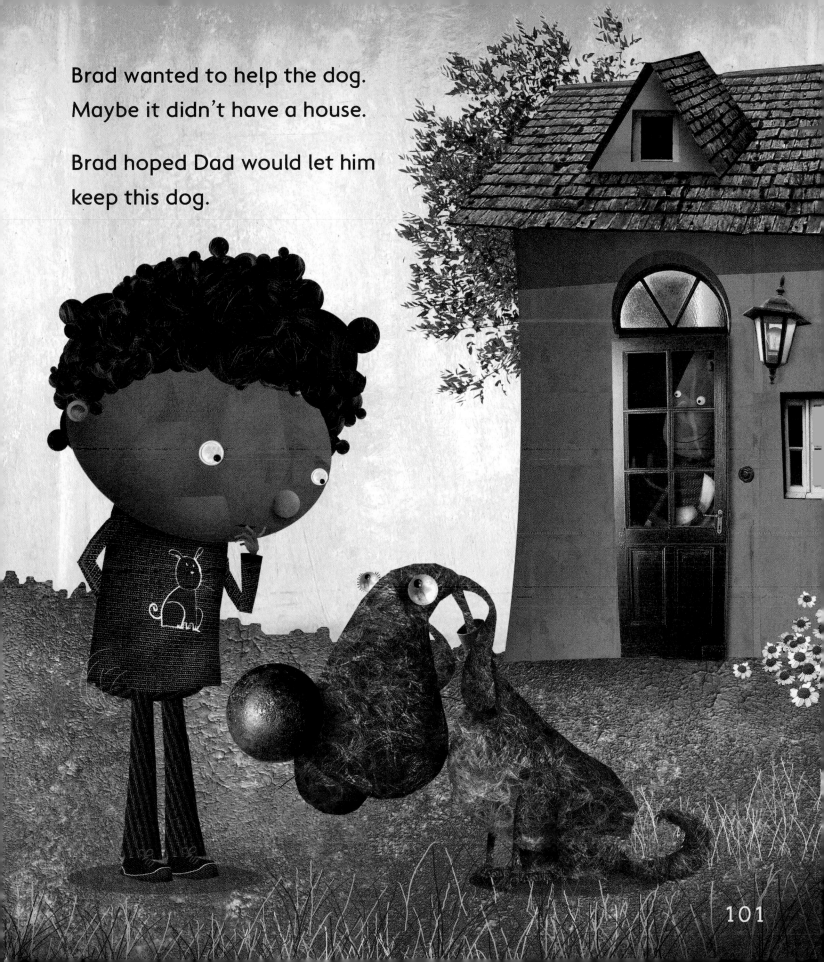

Then Dad came outside. How did you get here?" he asked.

"Do you know this dog?" Brad asked.

Dad nodded. "She lives down the road."

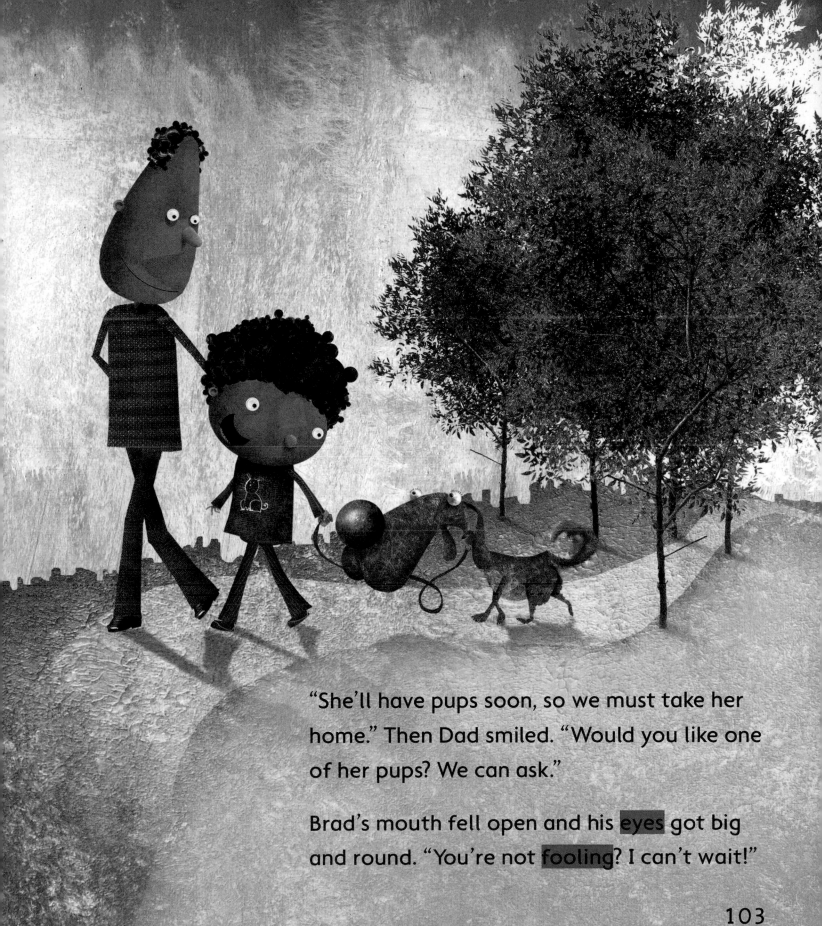

"She'll have pups soon, so we must take her home." Then Dad smiled. "Would you like one of her pups? We can ask."

Brad's mouth fell open and his eyes got big and round. "You're not fooling? I can't wait!"

Focus Skill

Plot, Setting, Characters

The **plot** is what happens in a story. The **setting** tells where and when a story takes place. The **characters** are the people and animals in a story.

In this picture the **plot** is about children visiting the king and queen. The **setting** is a castle in the daytime. The **characters** are the children, the king, and the queen.

104

Look at the picture. What is the plot? What is the setting? Who are the characters?

Try This!

Look at the picture. What is the plot? What is the setting? Who are the characters?

Words to Know

baby

heard

answered

pushed

pools

together

done

It was a nice day at the beach. A **baby** bird called for its mother. The mother **heard** and **answered**. The sea **pushed** a shell onto the sandy shore. The tide left **pools** of water in the sand. Two seals had fun playing **together** until the day was **done**.

 www.harcourtschool.com/storytown

Fiction

Genre Study

In **fiction** authors can tell a story through what the characters say to one another.

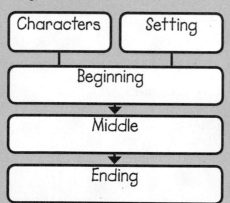

Characters	Setting
Beginning	
Middle	
Ending	

Comprehension Strategy

Monitor Comprehension: Make Inferences As you read, think about the clues that the author has left for you to think about.

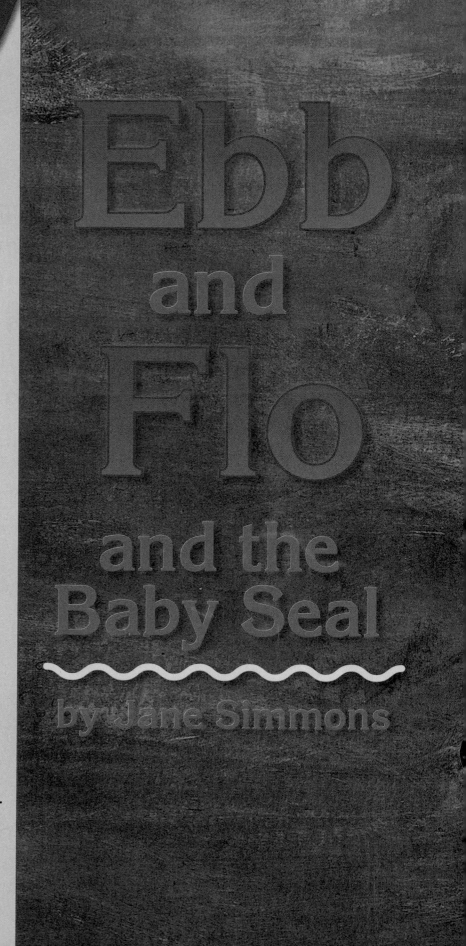

Ebb and Flo and the Baby Seal

by Jane Simmons

Ebb sat and listened to the rain and the wind.

Pitter, patter, pitter, patter, pitter, patter, whoosh!

Ebb had eaten all her biscuits and chewed her toy into little bits. She wanted someone to play with. *Woof!* said Ebb, but Flo was busy painting.

Woof! said Ebb, but Bird was busy chatting with the ducks.

Woof! said Ebb, but Mom was busy too.

So Ebb sat and listened to the wind and the rain.

Pitter, patter, pitter, patter, pitter, patter, whoosh!

Then she heard a cry from the beach. *Wah! Wah!*

It was a **baby** seal! At last
Ebb had someone to play with.
They played on the sand.

They played in the waves.

They played in the rock **pools**.
Ebb and the baby seal played all
day long.

As it got later, Ebb began to feel hungry.

But when she set off for home, the baby
seal tried to follow.

Wah! Wah! the baby seal cried.

Ebb stopped. *Woof!* she barked.

Why wouldn't the baby seal go home?

Ebb went to fetch help.

Woof! barked Ebb.

Beep! said Bird.

"Shush!" said Mom. "We're busy!"

Woof! WOOF! barked Ebb again, even louder.

"What's the matter, Ebb?" asked Flo.
WOOF! WOOF! WOOF! barked Ebb
until Flo and Mom followed her . . .

. . . all the way down to the beach.

"It's a baby seal," said Flo.

"Maybe she's hungry."

"Maybe she's lost," said Mom.

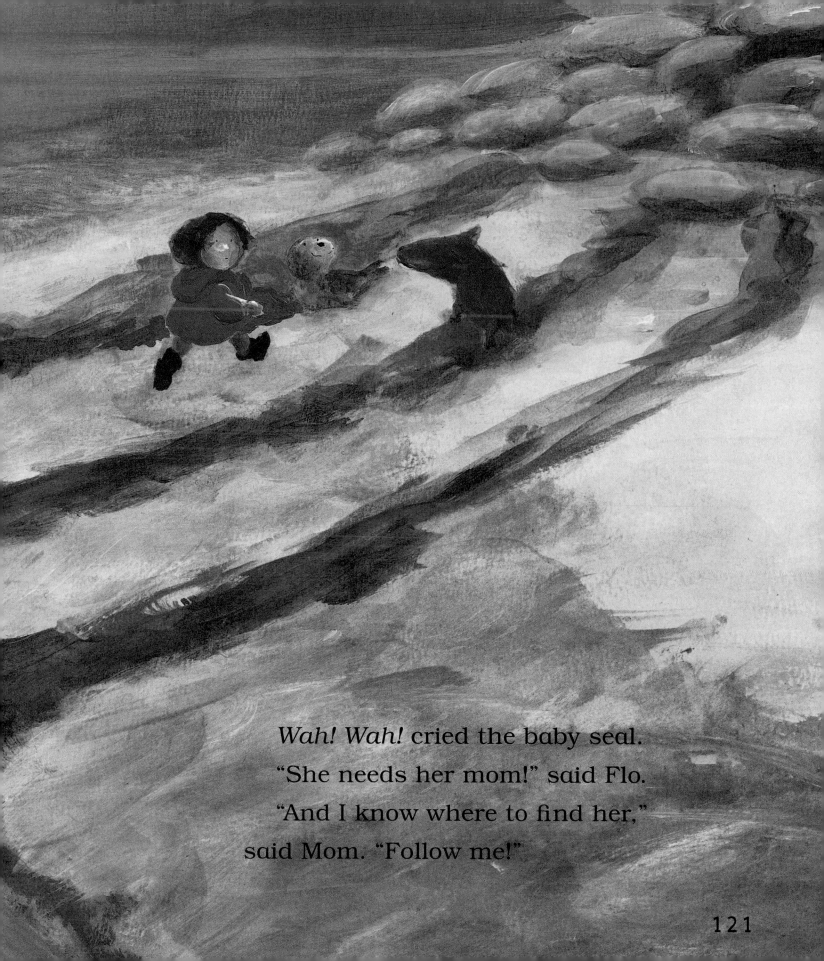

Wah! Wah! cried the baby seal.
"She needs her mom!" said Flo.
"And I know where to find her,"
said Mom. "Follow me!"

121

Flo followed Mom, Ebb followed
Flo, and the baby seal followed Ebb.

Wah! went the baby seal.

Flo heaved on the oars as Mom
pushed off.

Woof! said Ebb to the baby seal.

Wah! the baby seal cried back.

They rowed all the way out to
Seal Island.

Woof! Woof! barked Ebb.

Wah! went the baby seal.

There were seals everywhere.

"Oh, no!" said Flo. "We'll never find her mom!"

Ebb looked out to sea.

124

125

Suddenly Ebb saw a head bobbing all alone.

Woof! Woof! WOOF! Ebb barked as loud as she could.

Then they heard a loud *HOO!*

Wah! answered the baby seal.

"Ebb, you've found her mom!" said Flo.

The baby seal and her mother played together.

"Well done, Ebb," said Flo.

Woof! said Ebb.

Wah! Hoo! said the seals.

"Let's go home," said Mom.

That night, Ebb dreamed of the sea
and boats and seals.

*Pitter, patter, pitter, patter, pitter,
patter, whoosh!*

And far away there came a *Wah!
Hoo!* . . .

but Ebb was fast asleep.

Think Critically

1. What is the story's setting? 🦭 SETTING

2. How does Flo feel when she finds out the baby seal is lost? 🦭 CHARACTERS

3. What is the problem in the story? How is it solved? 🦭 PLOT

4. How can you tell that Ebb is a smart dog? MAKE INFERENCES

5. **WRITE** What would you have done to help the baby seal? 🖉 WRITING RESPONSE

Meet the Author/Illustrator
Jane Simmons

Jane Simmons lives on an old fishing boat. She and her husband and their pets travel to many interesting places. The interesting things she sees give her ideas for her books. She uses her computer on the boat to write her books and to stay in touch with people.

www.harcourtschool.com/storytown

133

Fellini
the Fur Seal

Hi! My name is Fellini. I am a fur seal.

I have lots of soft fur to keep me warm. I have flaps to cover my ears too. Can you see them? Some kinds of seals don't have ear flaps. Fur seals are special! I'm here to tell you more about us.

Fur seals live in cold places. We share our homes with other cold-loving animals. Some seals have penguins for neighbors. Would you like a penguin for a neighbor?

Mommy seals have babies in summer. Baby seals like me are called pups. When a mommy seal comes home, she calls for her pup. "Baaaa," she yells. That means "Come and eat!"

Someday I'll be as big as the daddy seal on this rock.

Now don't you agree fur seals are special?

135

Connections

Comparing Texts

1. How is the baby seal in the story like Fellini?

2. What other animals could you see at the beach?

3. Tell about an animal you have helped.

Writing

What if the baby seal could talk? Write what she would say to Ebb.

The baby seal would say "Thank you for

Phonics

Make and read new words.

Start with **shout**.

Take away the [s] [h].

Take away [u]. Change [t] to [w] [l]. Add [h] to the beginning. Take away [l].

Fluency Practice

Read the story with a partner. Take turns reading the pages. If your partner does not know a word, give help. Give your partner a "thumbs up" for reading words correctly.

Contents

Lesson 28

1 Get Started **Story**

Patty's Family Sketches

by Deanne W. Kells • illustrated by Melissa Iwai

2 Genre: Nonfiction

At the Crayon Factory

by Laura Williams

Crayons

written by Marchette Chute

illustrated by Vladimir Radunsky

3 Genre: Poetry

Phonics
Words with y
and ie

Words to Know

Review

toes

pushed

kinds

thought

answered

Patty's Family Sketches

by Deanne W. Kells

illustrated by
Melissa Iwai

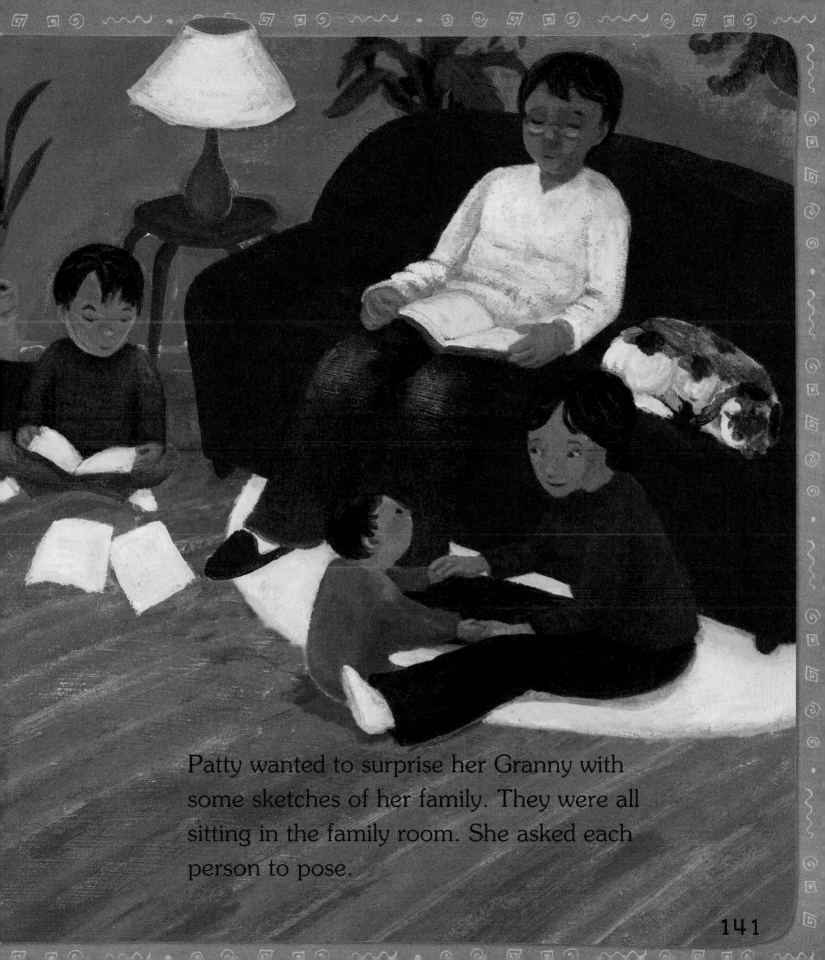

Patty wanted to surprise her Granny with some sketches of her family. They were all sitting in the family room. She asked each person to pose.

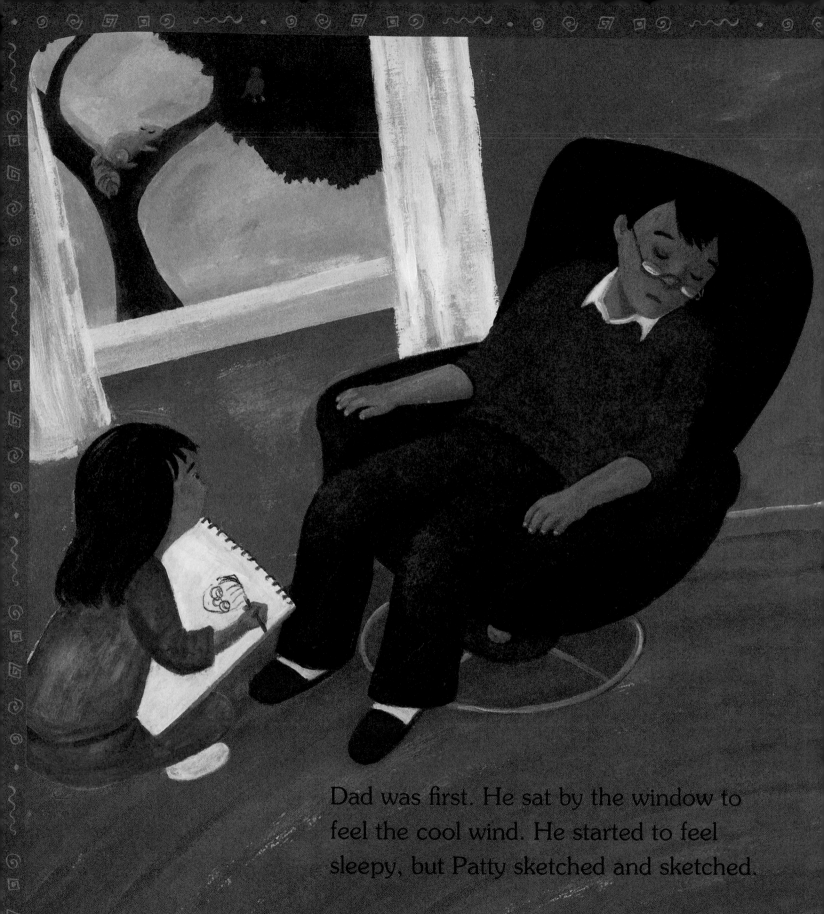

Dad was first. He sat by the window to feel the cool wind. He started to feel sleepy, but Patty sketched and sketched.

142

Mom was next. She was standing at the sink. She was smiling and posing for Patty. Her hands were soapy, but Patty sketched and sketched.

Charlie was playing ball in the backyard. He was clumsy, but Patty sketched and sketched.

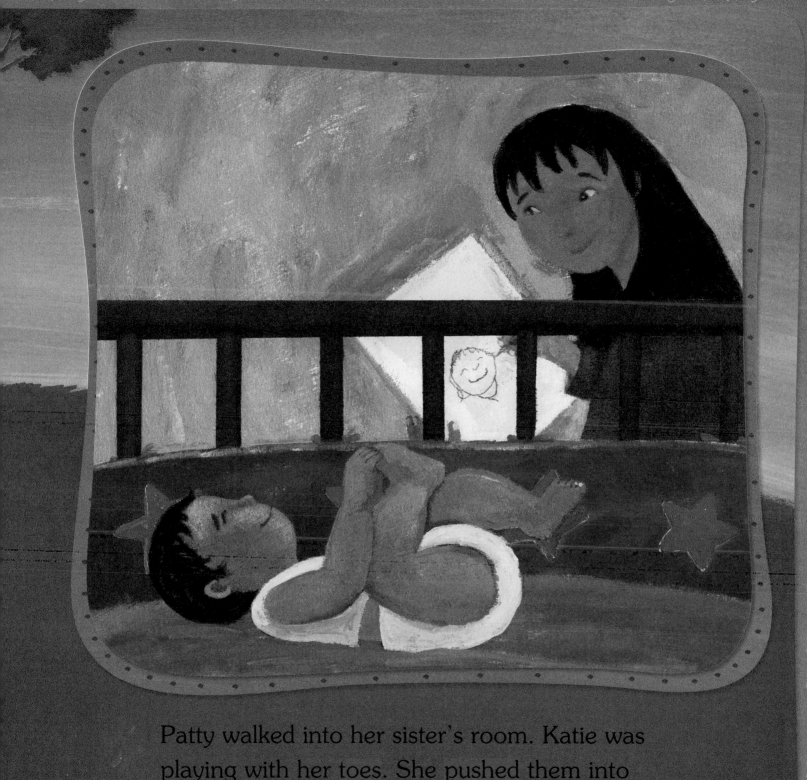

Patty walked into her sister's room. Katie was
playing with her toes. She pushed them into
the air and giggled. Katie wiggled a lot, but
Patty sketched and sketched.

Lucky was under the bed. All kinds of empty treat boxes sat beside him. Lucky was happy but very messy.

"What did you do?" thought Patty, but she sketched and sketched.

Patty gave her sketches to Granny. "This is
one silly family," said Patty.

"Well, I like silly families," answered Granny,
"and I really like this silly family!"

Focus Skill

 Details

Details are bits of information. They help answer the questions *Who? What? Where? When?*

This picture shows many details. They tell

Who? A boy and a man

What? flying a kite

Where? a city park

When? daytime

Look at the picture. What details do you see? Do they help answer the questions *Who? What? Where? When?*

Try This!

Look at the picture. What details do you see? Do they answer the questions *Who? What? Where? When?*

Words to Know

great

traveled

took

able

poured

blue

almost

We had a **great** time on our field trip today! We **traveled** to a crayon factory. We **took** a walk through the factory. We were **able** to see the workers make crayons. Some workers **poured** wax into molds. I liked the red crayons the best. Jan liked **blue**. We were so excited that we **almost** forgot to say thank you!

GO online www.harcourtschool.com/storytown

Genre Study

Some **nonfiction** selections use photos to give information. They often show things that happen in a certain order.

Comprehension Strategy

Monitor Comprehension: Reread When you don't understand something, read it again.

At the Crayon Factory

by Laura Williams

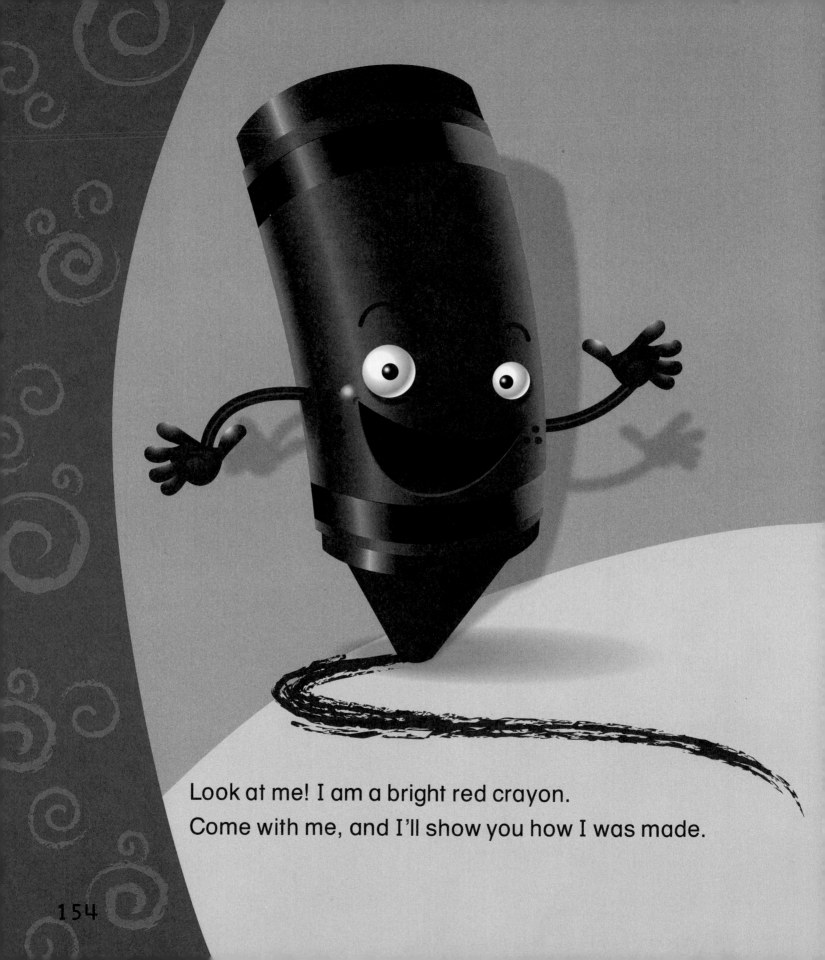

Look at me! I am a bright red crayon.
Come with me, and I'll show you how I was made.

It all started at a factory. First, I was part of a blob of wax. The wax is kept in some very large tanks. The tanks are very hot. Next, the wax flowed down a pipe. It went into a new tank.

Some red powder was added to the wax. Soon the wax turned red. I was very happy because red is my favorite color! The wax went down another pipe. It came out into a big bucket.

Then a worker poured the wax into a mold. The mold had many holes in it. Each hole was shaped like a crayon. Wax filled all the holes.

Cool water flowed around the mold. The water was chilly. It made the wax hard. I was almost a crayon!

A worker took me out of the mold. Other skinny, red crayons were all around me. The worker checked the crayons to see if some were chipped. Chipped crayons must be melted and made again.

At last, the worker checked me. He saw that I was not chipped. I was lucky because I didn't have to be melted again.

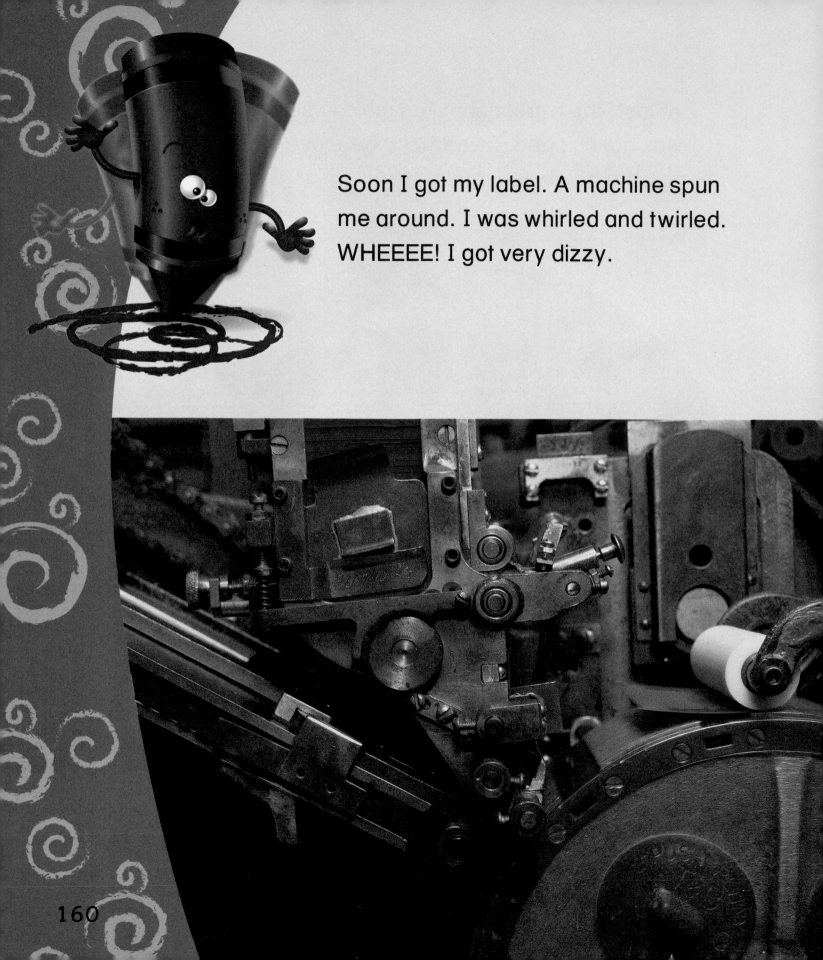

Soon I got my label. A machine spun me around. I was whirled and twirled. WHEEEE! I got very dizzy.

Next, a machine sorted us by color. There was a line for each color. I was in the red line.

Then I looked down and saw some more colors.

"Hello, Yellow and Green! Hello, Blue!" I called. "Hello, Red!" they called back. "Come down here and join us."

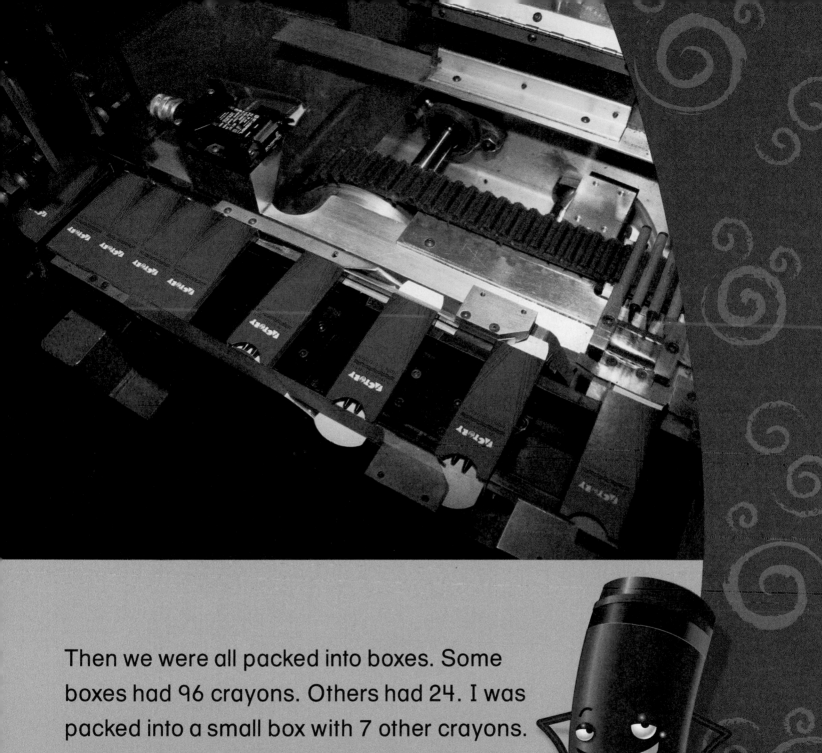

Then we were all packed into boxes. Some boxes had 96 crayons. Others had 24. I was packed into a small box with 7 other crayons. All the crayons were bright and friendly. We looked great together!

All the little boxes were packed into big boxes.
Workers loaded the big boxes onto a truck.
The truck traveled a long way. At last it
stopped at a store.

A worker placed us on a shelf. "Buy me! Buy me!" I called when people walked by.

One day, a girl in a red shirt picked up my box. Her name was Kelly. Now I would be able to color something!

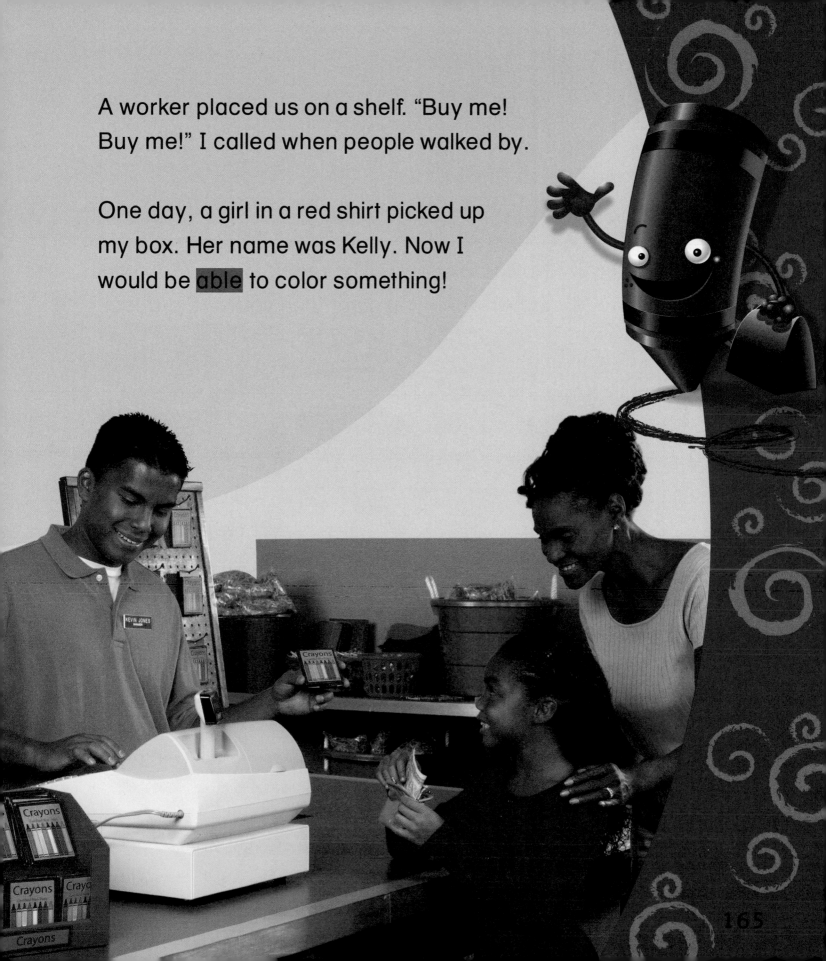

When Kelly and I got home, we colored some apples. The next day, we colored a beach ball. The best day of all was the day we colored a fire truck red!

Now you know how crayons are made. Think of me when you color with your red crayon!

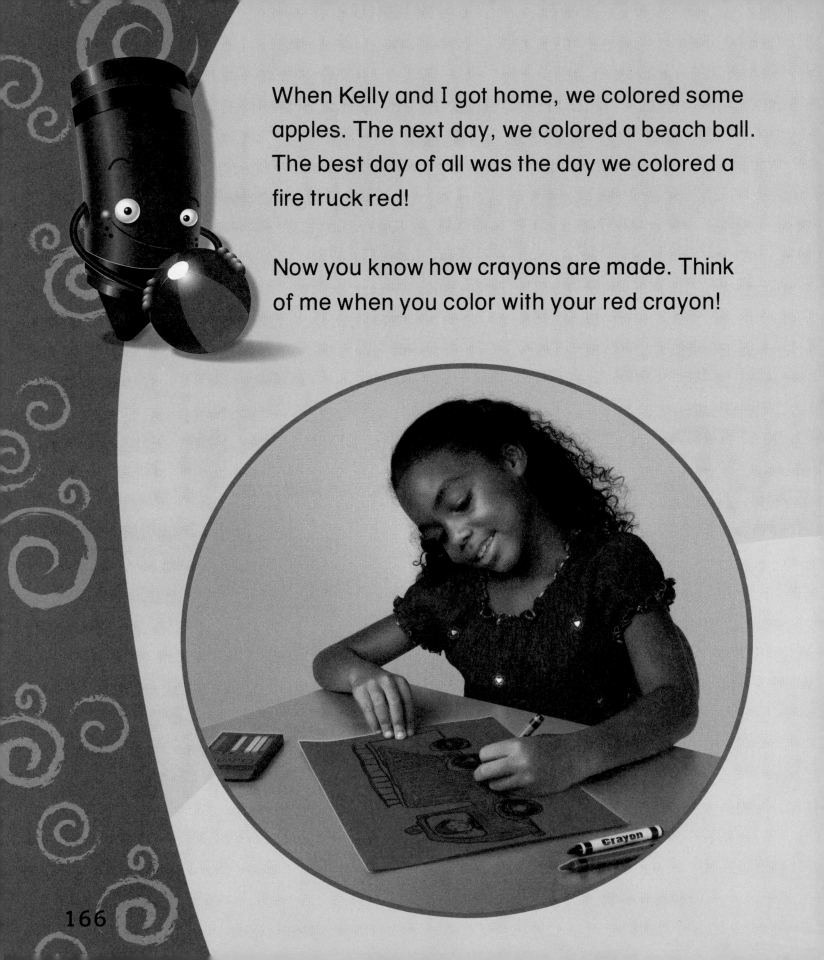

How to Make a Crayon

STEP 1

STEP 2

STEP 3

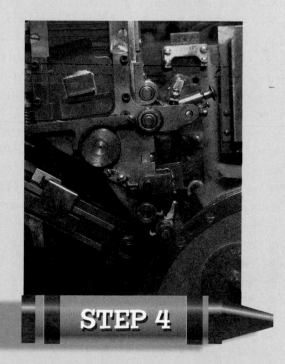

STEP 4

Think Critically

1 How does a crayon get its shape?

NOTE DETAILS

2 Does it take a lot of workers to make crayons? How do you know? DRAW CONCLUSIONS

3 How does a crayon get its color?

NOTE DETAILS

4 Why do you think the author chose a crayon character to tell the story?

MAKE INFERENCES

5 **WRITE** How is a crayon made? Tell how you know from the story.

Meet the Author
Laura Williams

Laura Williams has written many books for children. "I enjoyed writing this story because I learned new things," she says. "I never knew how crayons were made! I like crayons because when I use them, I feel like a child again. I like that feeling!"

Crayons

written by Marchette Chute

illustrated by Vladimir Radunsky

I've colored a picture with crayons.
　　I'm not very pleased with the sun.
I'd like it much stronger and brighter
　　And more like the actual one.
I've tried with the crayon that's yellow,
　　I've tried with the crayon that's red.
But none of it looks like the sunlight
　　I carry around in my head.

171

Connections

Comparing Texts

1. How are the story and the poem the same? How are they different?

2. What other things are made in a factory?

3. What crayon colors do you like? Why?

Writing

Think about a crayon that tells someone how to color a picture. Write what the crayon might say.

Pick me up and press me down on the paper.

Phonics

Make and read new words.

Start with **bunnies**.

Change **i** **e** **s** to **y**.

Change **b** to **s**.

Change **s** to **f**.

Change **n** **n** to **z** **z**.

Fluency Practice

Read the story with a partner. Take turns reading the pages. If your partner does not know a word, give some help. Give your partner a "thumbs up" for reading words correctly.

Contents

Lesson 29

Phonics
Words with <u>ew</u> and <u>oo</u>

Words to Know

Review

climbs

almost

push

pour

great

hears

A New Room by the Sea

by Deanne W. Kells

illustrated by Claudine Gevry

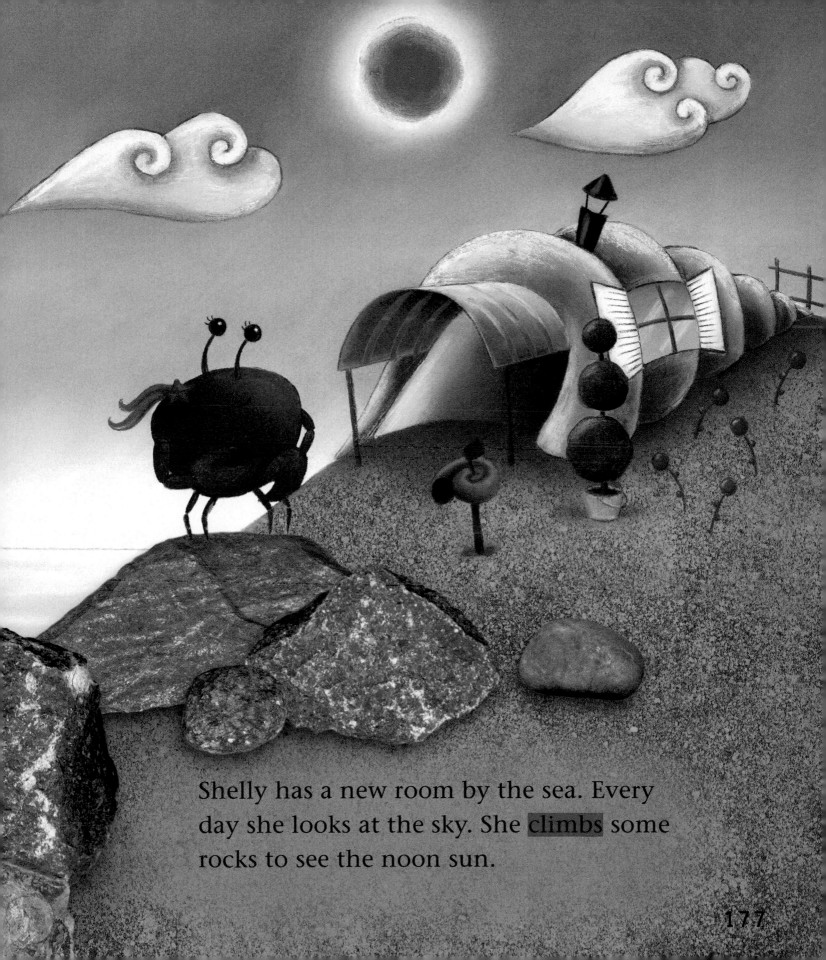

Shelly has a new room by the sea. Every
day she looks at the sky. She climbs some
rocks to see the noon sun.

The sun smiles on her garden. She digs in the dirt with her new tools. Almost every flower is blooming. The yellow ones shine like the sun.

The sky is cloudy and gloomy. The wind
swirls and whirls. WHOOSH! The sea
sparkles but is not smooth. The waves
push the sand like a broom!

Now it is rainy. Shelly bends over to see pools of water pour off the roof. The sky gets dark and the wind swoops in.

It is stormy. Shelly stays in her room.
She is making a warm scarf. Her eyes get
droopy and she starts to feel sleepy.

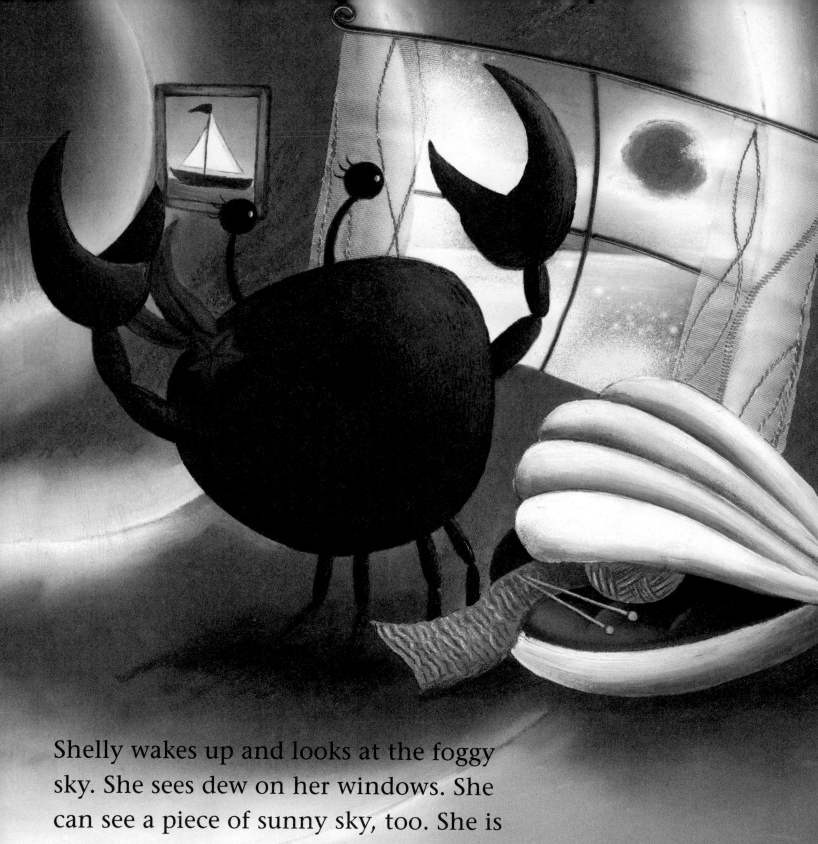

Shelly wakes up and looks at the foggy sky. She sees dew on her windows. She can see a piece of sunny sky, too. She is glad to see the sun again.

182

It is a beautiful day! Shelly puts on her boots and walks on the beach. She hears the sound of the waves, and she is happy. Shelly has a great new room by the sea!

Focus Skill

 Details

Details are bits of information. They help answer the questions *Who? What? When? Where?*

Look at the picture.

This picture shows many details. The details tell

Who? Lots of people

What? a parade

Where? a street in a town

When? daytime

Look at the picture. What details do you see? Do the details help answer the questions

Who?

What?

Where?

When?

Try This!

Look at the picture. What details do you see? Do they answer the questions *Who? What? Where? When?*

Words to Know

toward

boy

welcoming

building

tomorrow

186

This morning my friends and I headed **toward** the beach. We invited a new **boy** to come with us. Now I am making a **welcoming** sign for him. We will put it in front of the sand castle we are **building**. I hope the castle will still be here **tomorrow**!

 www.harcourtschool.com/storytown

Realistic Fiction

Genre Study
Realistic fiction stories sound as if they could happen in real life.

Beginning
↓
Middle
↓
Ending

Comprehension Strategy

Recognize Story Structure As you read, remember the order in which things happen. What happens at the beginning, in the middle, and at the end?

Sand Castle

by Brenda Shannon Yee
pictures by Thea Kliros

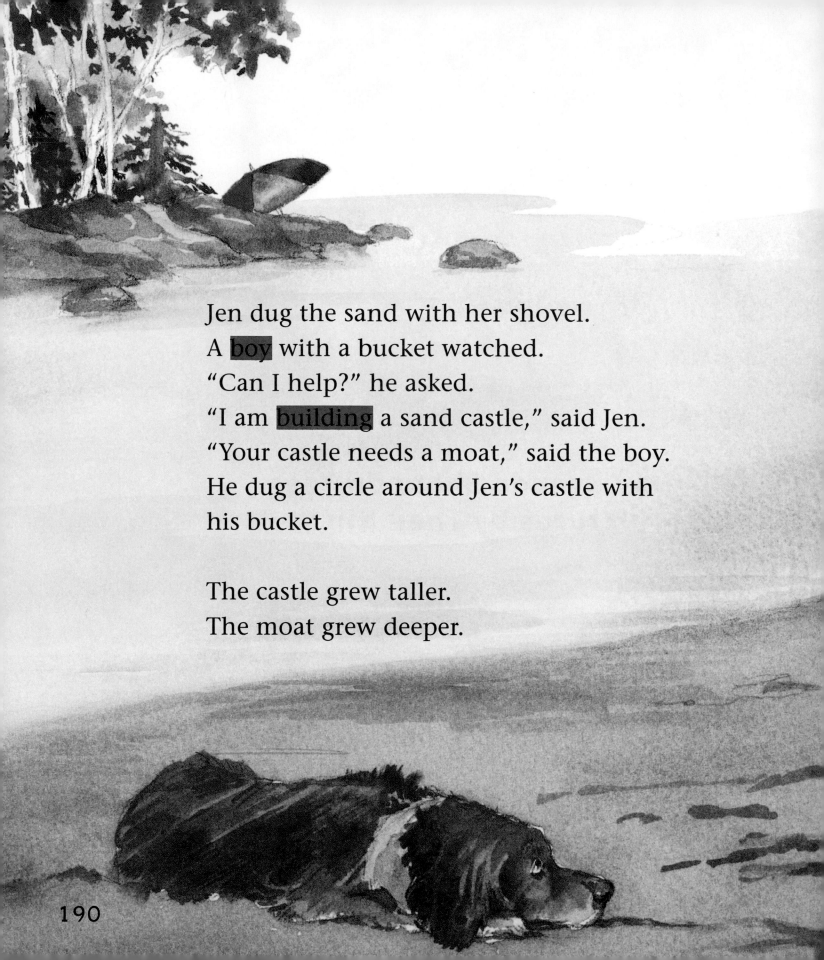

Jen dug the sand with her shovel.
A boy with a bucket watched.
"Can I help?" he asked.
"I am building a sand castle," said Jen.
"Your castle needs a moat," said the boy.
He dug a circle around Jen's castle with
his bucket.

The castle grew taller.
The moat grew deeper.

"Can I help?" asked a girl with a spoon.
"I am making the moat," said the boy.
"This is my castle," said Jen.

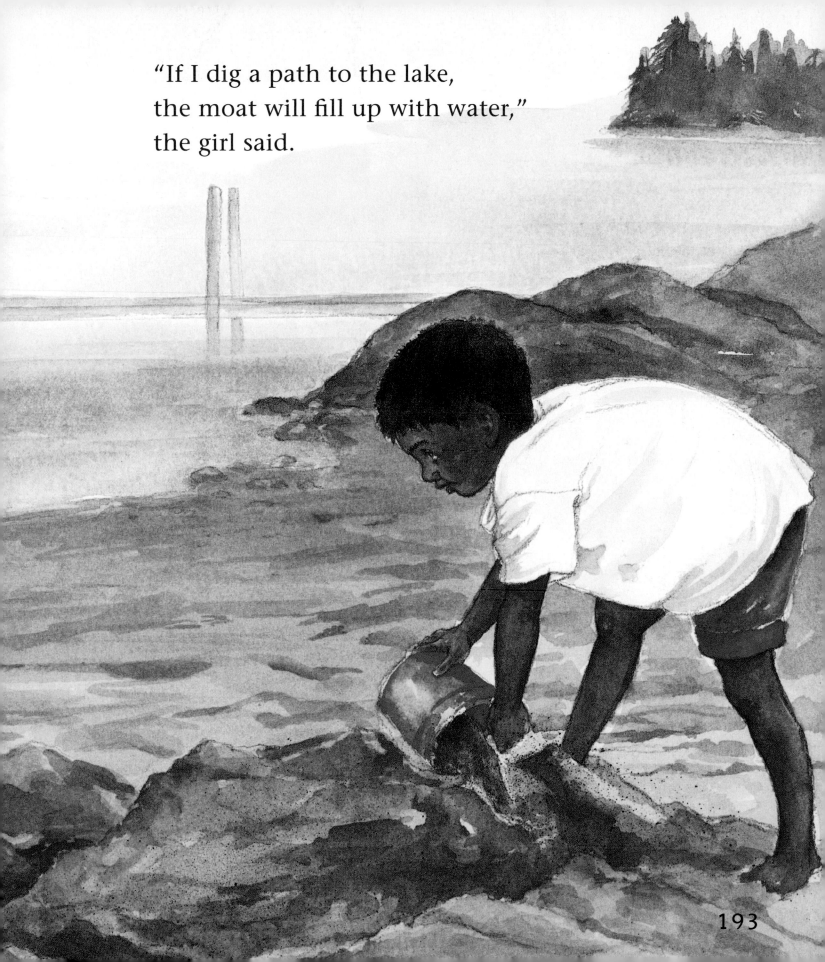

"If I dig a path to the lake,
the moat will fill up with water,"
the girl said.

193

She scooped a path in the sand.
Water sloshed into the path and
headed toward the moat.

The castle grew taller.
The moat grew deeper.
The path grew wider.

"Can I help?" asked a boy with a cup.
"I am digging the path to the water,"
said the girl.

196

"I am making the moat," said the boy.
"This is my castle," said Jen.

"You will need a wall to protect your
castle," said the boy with the cup.
The boy filled the cup with wet sand.
Pat, pat. He turned it over.
Tap, tap. One sand block stood.
Pat, tap. Two sand blocks.

The castle grew taller.
The moat grew deeper.
The path grew wider.
The wall grew longer.

"Can I help?" asked a girl holding a rake.

"I am building the wall," said the boy
with the cup.
"I am digging the path to the water,"
said the girl with the spoon.
"I am making the moat," said the boy
with the bucket.
"This is my castle," said Jen.

"You need a road, so people can get to the castle," said the girl with the rake. Dragging the rake in the sand, the girl traced a winding road. With the rake teeth, she swirled wavy shapes.

Hands patted and pushed the squishy sand.

The castle rose high.

The moat dipped deep.

The path flowed long.

The wall stood strong.

The road lay wide and welcoming.

Shadows stretched across the sand.
"Angela! Time to go!"
"Robert! We're leaving!"
"Tanisha! It's late!"
"Louis! Rinse your feet!"
"Jen! Say good-bye!"

"But what about the castle?
We worked so hard," Tanisha said.
"As soon as we leave, someone
will wreck it," said Louis.

"I know what to do!" Jen said.
Splat! She jumped on the castle.
In a flurry they all kicked the road,
toppled the wall, flattened the path,
filled the moat, and crushed the castle.

"Good-bye!" the beach friends shouted
as they scattered across the cooling sand.
"Let's do it again tomorrow!"

Think Critically

1 What does each child do to help build the sand castle? NOTE DETAILS

2 How can you tell the children work well together? MAKE INFERENCES

3 What makes you think that the children have just met? DRAW CONCLUSIONS

4 What causes the children to wreck the castle? CAUSE AND EFFECT

5 **WRITE** Write about something you made with some friends. WRITING RESPONSE

208

Meet the Author
Brenda Shannon Yee

Brenda Shannon Yee has been writing stories and poems since she was a little girl. This is her first picture book. Mrs. Yee loves to talk about her work. She often travels to schools to talk to children about it.

Meet the Illustrator
Thea Kliros

Thea Kliros was born in New York, but she has lived all over the world. She used colored pencils and watercolors to make the illustrations for this story.

 www.harcourtschool.com/storytown

Shape the Seashore

Every year, artists come to the beach to build sand sculptures. People come from all over the world to see them.

CALIFORNIA

Imperial Beach

210

Sand sculptures are works of art. Some sculptures are tiny. Others are huge. The biggest ones may take three days or more to finish!

First sand artists spray the sand with water. Next, they pack the wet sand tightly so it won't crumble. Then they are ready to start work.

Sand sculptures can look like almost anything. Think about what you could create with sand, water, and your dreams!

Connections

Comparing Texts

1 What happened at the beach in the story? What happened at the beach in the article?

2 What might you find at the beach?

3 What would you like to build out of sand?

Writing

Think about "Sand Castle." Now think about another way the story could end. Write a new ending to the story.

Another ending for Sand Castle could be

Phonics

Make and read new words.

Start with **boot**.

Change [b] to [r].

Add [d] to the beginning. Change [o] [o] [t] to [e] [w].

Change [d] [r] to [n].

Fluency Practice

Read the story aloud with a partner. Look for the part that begins with "The castle grew taller." Read the sentence that comes after this one a little bit faster. Then read the next sentences a bit faster still.

Contents

Lesson 30

1 Get Started **Story**

The Banjo Trick
by Linda Barr Illustrated by Ken Spengler

August Afternoon
by Marion Edey
Illustrated by Maria Carluccio
Genre: Poetry

2 Genre: Fantasy

Frog and Toad Together
by Arnold Lobel
An I CAN READ Book®

3

The Banjo Trick

by Linda Barr

illustrated by Ken Spengler

Duck was not happy swimming on his lake.
He told his friends, "Tomorrow I will look for
a way to be happy. Will you go with me?"

His friends were not so bold. They said, "No!"

Duck smiled. "I must go by myself, then."

The next day, Duck traveled for miles.
He saw Cat playing a golden banjo. "Are
you happy?" he asked Cat.

221

"Yes," Cat told him. "My banjo makes me happy."

"May I hold the banjo so I can be happy, too?" asked Duck.

"You can hold it for five gold pieces," answered Cat.

Duck felt so sad. "This is all the gold I have," he told Cat.

"Sold!" Cat smiled as he took Duck's gold.

"Thank you," Duck said. Then he held the banjo. "Wait! I feel the same as before."

"I don't," Cat told Duck. "I am happy to have five gold pieces."

"You tricked me! I'm done here. Keep this old banjo." Then Duck raced back to his lake.

When he got back, his friends asked,
"Are you happy now?"

"Yes," Duck told them. "I am most
happy when I am here with you!"

Phonics Skill

Words With Long Vowels i and o

The letter **i** can stand for the long <u>i</u> sound in the words **hi** and **tiger**.

hi

tiger

The letter **o** can stand for the long <u>o</u> sound in the words **cold** and **rolls**.

cold

rolls

224

**Look at each picture. Read the words.
Tell which word names the picture.**

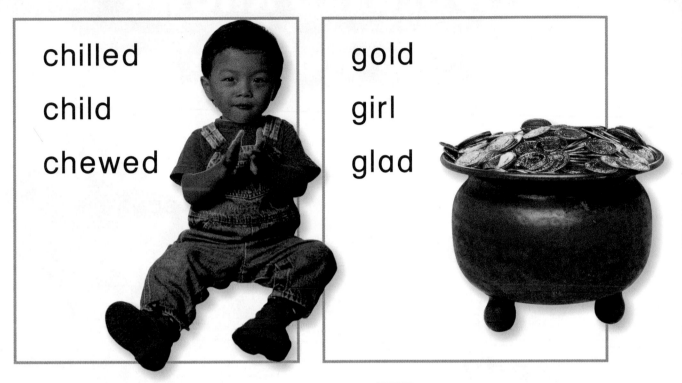

chilled

child

chewed

gold

girl

glad

GO online www.harcourtschool.com/storytown

Try This!

Read the sentences.

Mr. Gold is a baker. He owns
the old shop over on Mild
Street. He sells all kinds of rolls and
cakes. Most people go there a lot.
His rolls and cakes are so good!

Words to Know

any

nothing

sorry

ready

front

226

"Hi, Toad," said Frog. "Why do you look so sad?"

"I did not get any sleep last night," said Toad. "Nothing you can say will cheer me up."

"Oh," said Frog. "I'm sorry to hear that. I'll go back home. Just come over when you are ready to talk. We can sit out on my front porch."

"Thank you" said Toad. "I'll come after I rest a little bit."

Go online www.harcourtschool.com/storytown

Frog and Toad Together

by Arnold Lobel

An I CAN READ Book

Fantasy

Genre Study

A **fantasy** is a make-believe story. It might have funny things that happen at the beginning, middle, and ending.

Beginning

↓

Middle

↓

Ending

Comprehension Strategy

Summarize As you read, stop and think about what you have read so far.

Frog and Toad Together

by Arnold Lobel

A List

One morning Toad sat in bed.

"I have many things to do," he said.

"I will write them

all down on a list

so that I can remember them."

Toad wrote on a piece of paper:

A List of things to do today

Then he wrote:

Wake up

"I have done that," said Toad,

and he crossed out:

~~Wake up~~

Then Toad wrote other things
on the paper.

A List
of things to do
today

~~Wake up~~
Eat Breakfast
Get Dressed
Go to Frog's House
Take walk with Frog
Eat lunch
Take nap
Play games with Frog
Eat Supper
Go To Sleep

"There," said Toad.

"Now my day

is all written down."

He got out of bed

and had something to eat.

Then Toad crossed out:

~~Eat Breakfast~~

Toad took his clothes

out of the closet

and put them on.

Then he crossed out:

~~Get Dressed~~

Toad put the list in his pocket.

He opened the door

and walked out into the morning.

Soon Toad was at Frog's front door.

He took the list from his pocket

and crossed out:

Go to Frog's House

Toad knocked at the door.

"Hello," said Frog.

"Look at my list

of things to do,"

said Toad.

"Oh," said Frog,

"that is very nice."

Toad said, "My list tells me

that we will go

for a walk."

"All right," said Frog.

"I am ready."

Frog and Toad

went on a long walk.

Then Toad took the list

from his pocket again.

He crossed out:

~~Take walk with Frog~~

Just then there was a strong wind.

It blew the list out

of Toad's hand.

The list blew high up

into the air.

"Help!" cried Toad.

"My list is blowing away.

What will I do without my list?"

"Hurry!" said Frog.

"We will run and catch it."

"No!" shouted Toad.

"I cannot do that."

"Why not?" asked Frog.

"Because," wailed Toad,

"running after my list

is not one of the things

that I wrote

on my list of things to do!"

Frog ran after the list.

He ran over hills and swamps,

but the list blew on and on.

At last Frog came back to Toad.

"I am sorry," gasped Frog,

"but I could not catch

your list."

"Blah," said Toad.

"I cannot remember any of the things

that were on my list of things to do.

I will just have to sit here

and do nothing," said Toad.

Toad sat and did nothing.

Frog sat with him.

After a long time Frog said,

"Toad, it is getting dark.

We should be going to sleep now."

"Go to sleep!" shouted Toad.

"That was the last thing on my list!"

Toad wrote on the ground
with a stick: Go to sleep

Then he crossed out:

~~Go to sleep~~

"There," said Toad.

"Now my day

is all crossed out!"

"I am glad,"

said Frog.

Then Frog and Toad

went right to sleep.

Think Critically

1 Tell in a few sentences what the story is about. SUMMARIZE

2 How do you know that Frog is a good friend to Toad? DRAW CONCLUSIONS

3 Why didn't Toad try to get the list when it blew away? NOTE DETAILS

4 What makes you think that Toad is silly? MAKE INFERENCES

5 **WRITE** Write a list of the things you plan to do today. WRITING RESPONSE

About the Author and Illustrator
Arnold Lobel

Arnold Lobel said that when he was a child, checking books out from the library was one of his favorite things to do. He often wrote and illustrated stories to entertain his classmates.

When he began writing children's books, he sometimes got ideas from the cartoons his two children watched. Arnold Lobel wrote and illustrated many books that have become favorites of children everywhere.

 www.harcourtschool.com/storytown

August Afternoon

by Marion Edey
illustrated by Maria Carluccio

Where shall we go?
   What shall we play?
What shall we do
   On a hot summer day?

We'll sit in a swing.
   Go low. Go high.
And drink lemonade
   Till the glass is dry.

One straw for you,
   One straw for me,
In the cool green shade
   Of the walnut tree.

Connections

Comparing Texts

1 What do the story and the poem say about friendship?

2 How does doing something with a friend make it more fun?

3 What kinds of lists do you make?

Writing

Think about how Frog helped his friend Toad. Now think about a time you helped a friend. Write a short story about it.

One day my friend asked for help. I said, "Yes I will help you!"

252

Phonics

Make and read new words.

Start with **kind**.

Change **k** to **m** .

Change **n** to **l** .

Change **i** to **o** .

Take away the **m** .

Fluency Practice

Read the story aloud with a partner.
Take turns reading the pages. Imagine
that Toad speaks slowly. Read his parts
slowly. Imagine that Frog speaks more
quickly. Read his parts a bit more quickly.

Glossary

What Is a Glossary?

A glossary can help you read a word. You can

look up the word and read it in a sentence.

Some words have a picture to help you.

write   Jane likes to **write** letters.

A

a•ble   Bert is **able** to see his hand in the dark.

al•most   The boy **almost** fell off the curb.

an•swered   The children **answered** the teacher.

apples

an•y   Pick **any** book you would like to read.

ap•ples   Look at the basket of **apples.**

B

baby

ba•by   Josh is reading to his **baby** sister.

255

blue

building

blue   That is a **blue** butterfly.

boy   The **boy** has a red hat.

build•ing   That **building** is tall.

clear   The sky is **clear**.

climbed   Nick and Kate **climbed** to the
top of the tree.

col•or   Red is a **color**.

cray•ons The **crayons** are red, yellow, and blue.

crayons

D
---

done I'll call you when I'm **done** eating.

E

Earth This shows **Earth** from space.

Earth

F
---

fool•ing Stop **fooling** around!

front She sits in the **front** of the class.

hair

helmet

G

good-bye   The girl said **good-bye** when she left.

great   The children had a **great** trip to the beach.

H

hair   He is getting his **hair** cut.

heard   I **heard** a tap on the door.

hel•met   He wears his **helmet** when he rides his bike.

K

kinds   There are many **kinds** of animals.

N

noth•ing   There is **nothing** to do in this empty room.

O

on•ly   We **only** have one pet.

P

pools   There are **pools** of water around the sink.

poured

quills

table

poured   I **poured** milk in Ken's cup.

pushed   The teacher **pushed** her desk to the wall.

---Q---

quills   Watch out for those sharp **quills**!

---R---

read•y   Is Dennis **ready** for bed?

---T---

ta•ble   This family is reading at the **table**.

thought   I **thought** it was time to go.

toes   She can tap her **toes.**

to•geth•er   The sisters play **together**.

to•mor•row   It will snow **tomorrow**.

took   The children **took** their work home.

to•ward   Ray lifts his head **toward** the sky.

trav•eled   We **traveled** to visit my uncle.

toes

together

traveled

Acknowledgments

For permission to reprint copyrighted material, grateful acknowledgment is made to the following sources:

HarperCollins Publishers: "A List" from *Frog and Toad Together* by Arnold Lobel. Copyright © 1971, 1972 by Arnold Lobel. *Sand Castle* by Brenda Shannon Yee, illustrated by Thea Kliros. Text copyright © 1999 by Brenda Shannon Yee; illustrations copyright © 1999 by Thea Kliros.

Elizabeth Hauser: "Crayons" from *Rhymes About Us* by Marchette Chute. Published by E. P. Dutton & Co., 1974.

Margaret K. McElderry Books, an Imprint of Simon & Schuster Children's Publishing Division: Ebb & Flo and the Baby Seal by Jane Simmons. Copyright © 2000 by Jane Simmons.

Scribner, an imprint of Simon & Schuster Adult Publishing Group: "The Little Turtle" from *Collected Poems,* Revised Edition by Vachel Lindsay. Text copyright 1925 by The Macmillan Company; text copyright renewed 1948 by Elizabeth C. Lindsay.

Photo Credits

Placement Key: (t) top; (b) bottom; (l) left; (r) right; (c) center; (bg) background; (fg) foreground; (i) inset

12 (t) Jane Wooster Scott/SuperStock; 24 (c) Atlantide Phototravel/Corbis; 24 (br) PhotoDisc/Getty Images; 25 (c) PhotoDisc/Getty Images; 26 Wayne Lynch/Masterfile; 28 (t) Wayne Lynch/Masterfile; 28 (b) Paul Hanna/Reuters/Corbis; 29 (r) Byron Jorjorian/Digital Vision/Getty Images; 30 (bl) Wayne Lynch/Masterfile; 30 (tl) Gerry Ellis/Minden Pictures; 30 (tr) GK Hart/Vikki Hart/The Image Bank/Getty Images; 30 (br) Paul Hanna/Reuters/Corbis; 31 (c) Wayne Lynch/Masterfile; 32 (r) David Trood/Getty Images; 32 (c) Steve Bloom; 33 (c) Art Wolfe, Inc.; 34 (c) Thai-Images/Alamy; 35 (c) Jose Fuste Raga/Corbis; 36 (c) Gerry Ellis/Minden Pictures; 36 (r) Kevin Leigh/Index Stock Imagery, Inc.; 37 (c) GK Hart/Vikki Hart/The Image Bank/Getty Images; 38 (c) Hans Reinhard/Bruce Coleman USA; 38 (r) Jim Wehtje/Brand X Pictures/PictureQuest; 39 (c) Anup Shah/Taxi/Getty Images; 40 (c) age fotostock/SuperStock; 40 (r) Seide Preis/Getty Images; 41 (r) GK Hart/Vicki Hart/Getty Images; 41 (c) Tom Brakefield/Bruce Coleman, Inc.; 42 (c) Londolozi/Masterfile; 42 (r) GK Hart/Vicki Hart/Getty Images; 43 (c) David A. Northcott/Corbis; 43 (r) David A. Northcott/Corbis; 44 (r) David A. Northcott/Corbis; 44 (c) Dwight Kuhn Photography; 45 (c) Paul Hanna/Reuters/Corbis; 46 (c) Jeff Rotman/Stone/Getty Images; 46 (r) Paul Hanna/Reuters/Corbis; 48 (bg) Photodisc/Getty Images; 49 (l) Byron Jorjorian/Digital Vision/Getty Images; 52 Royalty-Free/Corbis; 58 (r) The Stocktrek Corp/PictureQuest; 90 (br) Neil Armstrong/NASA/Corbis; 90 (t) CSA Plastock / Getty Images; 91 (tr) © Carphotos/Alamy; 91 (tl) © Dennis Frates/Alamy; 91 (bl) © Skyscan Photo Library / Alamy; 91 (cl) Corbis; 91 (cr) Larry Fisher / Masterfile; 91 (br) Leon Neal/Stringer/Getty Images; 93 (cr) PhotoDisc/Getty Images; 106 emily2k/Shutterstock; 134 (bl) Ron Levy/Global Image Group; 135 (bl) Galen & Barbara Rowell/Mountain Light; 135 (cr) Kim Heacox/Peter Arnold, Inc.; 135 (bc) Ron Levy/Global Image Group; 135 (tl) Steve Bloom Images/Alamy; 137 (tr) George Doyle/Stockdisc Classic/Getty Images; 148 (c) Photodisc Green/Getty Images; 150 Gale Zucker Photography; 155 Gale Zucker; 156 Gale Zucker Photography; 157 (t) Gale Zucker Photography; 157 (b) Gale Zucker Photography; 158 (t) Gale Zucker Photography; 159 (b) Gale Zucker Photography; 160 (b) Gale Zucker Photography; 161 (t) Gale Zucker Photography; 162 (b) Gale Zucker Photography; 163 (t) Gale Zucker Photography; 164 (t) Royalty-Free/Corbis; 167 (tl) Gale Zucker Photography; 167 Gale Zucker Photography; 167 Gale Zucker Photography; 167 Gale Zucker Photography; 185 (tr) Richard Hutchings/PhotoEdit; 210 (bg) Charles Hester Photography; 210 (c) Joseph Baraty; 210 (bg) South Padre Island, Texas Convention & Visitors Bureau; 211 (tl) Charles Hester Photography; 211 (cr) Charles Hester Photography; 211 (bl) Charles Hester Photography; 211 (tl) Joseph Baraty; 211 (cr) Joseph Baraty; 211 (tl) South Padre Island, Texas Convention & Visitors Bureau; 211 (cr) South Padre Island, Texas Convention & Visitors Bureau; 211 (bl) South Padre Island, Texas Convention & Visitors Bureau; 224 (br) Brand X/SuperStock; 224 (t) Joseph Calev/Shutterstock; 225 (br) Chuck Pefley/Alamy Images; 226 Djordje Zoric/Shutterstock.

All other photos © Harcourt School Publishers. Harcourt photos provided by Harcourt Index, Harcourt IPR, and Harcourt Photographers: Weronica Ankarorn, Eric Camden, Doug DuKane, Ken Kinsie, April Riehm and Steve Williams.

Illustration Credits

Cover Art; Laura and Eric Ovresat, Artlab, Inc.